Making Your Church Sustainable

Making Your Church Sustainable

A Practical Guide

Nigel Walter

CANTERBURY
PRESS
Norwich

© Nigel Walter 2024

First published in 2024 by the Canterbury Press Norwich
Editorial office
3rd Floor, Invicta House
110 Golden Lane
London EC1Y 0TG, UK
www.canterburypress.co.uk

Canterbury Press is an imprint of Hymns Ancient & Modern Ltd
(a registered charity)

Hymns Ancient & Modern® is a registered trademark of
Hymns Ancient & Modern Ltd
13A Hellesdon Park Road, Norwich,
Norfolk NR6 5DR, UK

British Library Cataloguing in Publication data

A catalogue record for this book is available
from the British Library

ISBN: 978 1 78622 497 2

Typeset by Regent Typesetting

Contents

Part 2 Technologies

Part 3 Processes

Acknowledgements

Like many of us, I was not brought up with much awareness of the importance of sustainability. For the most part, I've had to learn it, and this learning has mostly happened in dialogue with others. I would particularly like to thank Catherine Ross, Open and Sustainable Churches Officer and then Net Zero Carbon Senior Projects Manager at the Church of England until 2023, who was responsible for developing the Practical Path to Net Zero Carbon, among many other tools and initiatives, and from whom, in working together, I have learned so much.

A number of people kindly commented on a draft of this book, and I would particularly like to thank Mel Allwood, Ruth Chamberlain, Nigel Cooper, Tobit Curteis, Mike Dyer, David Knight, Hilary Marlow, Kathy Ogilvie, David Ogilvie, Apos Petrakis, Simon Pugh-Jones, Andrew Shepherd, Robert Skelton and Luke Tatam. Their input has helped hugely in terms of both detail and overall balance, and various indiscretions have been avoided! Any remaining errors are entirely down to me.

I am grateful to professional colleagues at the Ecclesiastical Architects and Surveyors Association (EASA) for providing a forum for discussion – some parts of the book are drawn from articles I have contributed to the *EASA Journal*. Tom Crooks provided the photo of the Cemetery Road PV panels. Thanks also to colleagues on the Ely Diocesan Environmental Task Group, including the late Jenny Gage, for progressing the sustainability agenda in this particular neck of the woods.

And finally, my thanks go to all those involved with Archangel Architects, whether colleagues, consultants or clients, for their support, their contributions, and their trust.

Nigel Walter
nw@archangelarchitects.co.uk

Abbreviations

ASHP	air source heat pump
CBC	Church Buildings Council
CfGA	Caring for God's Acre
CIBSE	Chartered Institution of Building Services Engineers
CoP	Coefficient of Performance
DAC	Diocesan Advisory Committee
DCMS	Department for Culture, Media and Sport
DEO	diocesan environmental officer
EASA	Ecclesiastical Architects and Surveyors Association
EV	electric vehicle
FIR	far infrared radiation
FIT	Feed-in Tariffs scheme
GSHP	ground source heat pump
HVO	hydrogenated vegetable oil
kWp	kilowatt peak (rating of PV panels)
LED	light emitting diode
M&E	mechanical and electrical (engineer, services, etc.)
NZC	net zero carbon
PPNZC	Practical Path to Net Zero Carbon
PV	photovoltaic (panels)
QI	Quinquennial Inspection
SCoP/SPF	Seasonal Coefficient of Performance/Seasonal Performance Factor
SPAB	Society for the Protection of Ancient Buildings
TRV	thermostatic radiator valve
ZEB®	Zero Emission Boiler (Tepeo)

Preface

In responding to the climate crisis, church communities are increasingly asking what they can and should do with their buildings to make them more sustainable. This book will help answer that question. Buildings and sustainability can both be seen as very technical subjects; this book (like the earlier *Buildings for Mission*)[1] aims to demystify the topic and to equip non-professionals with a basic framework of understanding to help them engage positively with professional advisers and the relevant permissions processes. To manage your expectations, given the scope and complexity of the topic, a book like this can at best offer an introduction. But I hope it will give you sufficient information – including, importantly, the principles behind the issues in question – to be of real practical help in working through your response to the climate crisis.

'Sustainability' is a big word. One well-recognized definition defines it as meeting the needs of the present without compromising the ability of future generations to meet their own needs (more on this in Chapter 1). On this definition, sustainability is all about balance between generations, in contrast to our modern tendency to spend the world's resources as if there were no tomorrow. The Church sees itself as 'the communion of saints', a community that is not only worldwide, but also spread across time, combining present, past and (by implication) future generations. We should see sustainability as a profoundly Christian concern, and be striving for this balance in all that we do.

At a national level, buildings are responsible for a very substantial proportion of energy demand – around 40% of the total – and therefore are a major source of carbon emissions. If we are to contain the effects of human-induced global warming/heating within 'acceptable' limits, addressing the carbon footprint of our buildings (in both their construction and use) is central to whether we succeed or fail. There are, of course, significant *lifestyle* issues we should urgently attend to, such as what we eat and how and where we travel; so, with its focus on buildings, this book can address only part of a much larger picture. But, because of the public and communal nature of church buildings, and because of the heritage sensitivity of many of them, they are an important part of that wider picture.

It is important to frame what follows by clarifying the viewpoint from which I am writing. I am a Specialist Conservation Architect leading a practice based in East Anglia. I am an inspecting architect for some 75 church buildings, mostly listed and many medieval. My architectural practice, Archangel, also undertakes alteration projects to church buildings, and occasionally builds new ones, across a range of denominations. Since 2016 I have had the privilege of serving on the Church of England's Church Buildings Council, where I have witnessed and contributed to policy development on improving the sustainability of church buildings. And outside of work I am a Licensed Lay Minister in my local church, so have first-hand experience of how churches work as both community and building. This book draws on all of that experience.

I should also say that in my professional practice as an architect I have moved a long way in my approach to the issue of sustainability – looking back, I now wonder what took me so long. Meanwhile, the specific technologies that help us address the climate crisis continue to develop at pace, which means that parts of this book will no doubt soon be superseded. That is a good thing, and to be expected, because we are living through a time of significant change. I look forward to a time when this book as a whole becomes irrelevant, when net zero carbon has become the norm for churches. Clearly that is a good way off, but it is the goal to which we must all strive. So, to work!

Note

1 Nigel Walter and Andrew Mottram, *Buildings for Mission: A Complete Guide to the Care, Conservation and Development of Churches*, Norwich: Canterbury Press, 2015.

Introduction: Where to Begin

Responding to the Climate Crisis

We are living in a time of change, which is both daunting and exciting. Chief among these changes is the growing realization that current human behaviour is unsustainable in the long term. Ecologists have long warned that collectively we are putting far too great a burden on the created world and its complex systems, and the effects of this are becoming increasingly evident. We are facing an existential crisis – if we do not rethink and change our ways (repent, in theological terms), then our very existence is in serious doubt. Yes, we face a climate *crisis*.

This crisis should not be 'new news' – we have known about global heating for a very long time. A short report from the *Rodney and Otamatea Times* (New Zealand) was recently dug out of the archives (and went viral):

COAL CONSUMPTION AFFECTING CLIMATE. The furnaces of the world are now burning about 2,000,000,000 tons of coal a year. When this is burned, uniting with oxygen, it adds about 7,000,000,000 tons of carbon dioxide to the atmosphere yearly. This tends to make the air a more effective blanket for the earth and to raise its temperature. The effect may be considerable in a few centuries.

The date of the article? 14 August 1912! Yes, we have known about global heating for a *very* long time, it's just that we have generally chosen not to pay attention.

Now that we are finally paying attention, the culture around sustainability – the way it is viewed across society, and what sorts of change we might make to our buildings – is shifting rapidly.

The hosting of the UN's COP26 Climate Change Conference in Glasgow in late 2021 has helped with that cultural shift, raising the sense of urgency, both nationally and globally.

In February 2020, almost two years before COP26, the Church of England General Synod committed to a carbon reduction target of net zero by 2030.[1] Several other denominations have adopted similar targets, generally with longer time frames. The target of 2030 is hugely ambitious, but one I would argue that is appropriate in the face of the climate crisis. Summing up the Synod debate, the Bishop of Salisbury described the 2030 target as 'a game changer'. Assuming steady progress during 2020–30, this target requires a 26% reduction in carbon emissions in each and every one of those ten years.[2] Even if action had started straight away that was a huge commitment, but how many of our churches have even begun to make progress?

There is a very real question of where the money will come from for all this change. While this book cannot provide guidance on grant funding, I would note that grant funders are also reviewing their priorities in the face of the sustainability challenge, so there is change here too. I would hope that central government would soon provide much greater financial support, to match its declared intention to transition the economy onto a greener footing.

In addition to funding, since many of our church buildings are historic and protected, there is also a substantial issue around what sorts of change the permissions system will allow. The climate crisis and the challenge of that 2030 target have significant implications for how we hold heritage and environmental concerns together – more on this in Chapter 6.

I hope all this doesn't leave you miserable. We shouldn't – indeed we mustn't – despair! Yes, we need to take this situation with the utmost seriousness; and yes, we need to face our responsibilities – to God's creation, and to those in other nations now paying the very real price of our excesses. But we should do so *with hope*. Not least because, as I trust will become clear in what follows, alongside or within this great responsibility there is also a rich seam of opportunity.

The Audience for this Book

This book is primarily addressed to the UK's estimated 39,000 church communities who are wrestling with how to respond to the climate crisis. Clearly, with such a wide audience, not everything in these pages will be directly applicable to all – so please read flexibly, and if you feel a section is not relevant, then it can be skipped.

While the intended audience is broad, some of the content relates specifically to Church of England churches, and there are several reasons for this. First, there is representation – of all those UK churches, some 40% are Church of England buildings. Second, the Church of England was early in setting its ambitious target of reaching net zero carbon by 2030, and as a result has been leading in the development of a wide range of resources for church communities. Third, of all church buildings, it is the historic ones that are (at least on the face of it) trickiest to deal with, and the significant majority of those are Anglican buildings.[3] Finally, Church of England buildings account for a good proportion of my experience.

It should also be stated that this book is written from an unapologetically Christian point of view, by someone who sees his faith informing and shaping his professional life. A key aspect of sustainability is taking the holistic view. For Christians, this means we cannot ignore the theology, but must keep it embedded in all our decision making. While much of what follows, especially in the later chapters, concerns technologies and processes, the theology should remain central.

All of that said, it is clear that not everyone enjoys or sees the relevance of Christian theology. Even so, I would hope that others coming from different perspectives who engage with this book would find useful material here, including in the referenced resources. I'm thinking, for example, of those responsible for secular historic buildings, or other community buildings such as village halls, those of other faiths, or indeed those with no religious faith who are involved in their communities, and perhaps responsible for community buildings. And that reflects another aspect of sustainability, that no one group of people can hope to address the climate crisis on their own – we have to build the broadest possible coalition if we are to have any chance of success. Which, of course, is part of that rich seam of opportunity mentioned above.

Some who pick up this book will be aware of the successful Eco Church scheme run by the Christian environmental charity, A Rocha UK, or the similar schemes run by Eco-Congregation in Scotland and Northern Ireland. These schemes are an excellent tool for encouraging a broad engagement with sustainability and for raising ambition, and they have seen good take-up by church communities and denominational structures. The Eco Church scheme is outlined in Chapter 3. While buildings form one of Eco Church's five areas of focus a general tool such as this clearly cannot go into any detail; this book aims to complement Eco Church by giving more specific guidance within the narrower focus of buildings, with the aim of giving church communities the knowledge and tools to understand what is achievable in their given situation.

A Question of Timing

So, why produce a book like this now? In one sense, the sooner the better – there is much greater awareness now among churches, and an increasing desire to take action. In a Church of England context, we are already more than a third of the way on our journey from 2020 to 2030, so it is good for church communities to look at what carbon reduction we have achieved, and whether we have a credible plan to reach net zero carbon (see Chapter 3 for the Net Zero Carbon Routemap).

By the same token, because things are changing rapidly, a book on sustainability carries the clear risk of rapidly becoming out of date. This is particularly the case when it comes to the specific technologies discussed in Chapter 4. It is also the case that there is limited value in replicating good material that is already available in other forms. The strategy adopted in this book is therefore to provide an introduction to the landscape and an overall map of how these technologies might fit into the broader picture, and then to signpost the reader to other sources of material via web links – acknowledging that these, of course, also go out of date.

While a book like this can never answer every question, by providing a framework and by offering outline guidance it can perhaps help churches to ask better questions and make progress towards becoming fully sustainable.

Outline of the Book

The book is divided into three main parts: Principles, Technologies and Processes.

Part 1, Principles, takes an overview of sustainability. It begins in Chapter 1 by reflecting on the interrelation of sustainability with theology and mission, and then goes on in Chapter 2 to discuss some general principles of how to approach sustainability and buildings. Chapter 3 introduces some tools that help churches to plan in an appropriate manner.

Part 2, Technologies, forms the central third of the book in Chapter 4, discussing a range of technologies that churches may consider, and others that should be treated more sceptically.

Part 3, Processes, looks at professional advisers in Chapter 5, and at what is involved in getting permission in Chapter 6, particularly in the case of listed historic buildings.

Finally, the Conclusion draws the various threads of the book together. There is then a Resources section, which signposts users to other available guidance, and an Appendix.

Terminology

I will close this introduction by visiting three key terms, and explaining how and why they are used.

'**Climate crisis**' describes how the climate is changing due to the choices humanity has made, particularly since the Industrial Revolution. And yes, this is a crisis for the world. There are two issues here. First, the impact of this crisis is unevenly spread, with the world's poor and vulnerable bearing the brunt. Second, this is a crisis that is unfolding over time; just because we haven't yet felt its full force, doesn't mean that all is well, because of the momentum that climate change has already gained. It is important to note that almost all of the change in global temperatures that we have seen 'since pre-industrial times' has come in the last 50 years.

'**Global warming**' is another well-used term. The problem here is that in terms of personal comfort, warmth is often a good thing, particularly in a cold climate. In July 2023, UN secretary-general António Guterres declared that 'the era of global boiling has arrived', after new record temperatures were set. While 'global boiling' is helpful in communicating the seriousness of the situation, it perhaps stretches credibility for those not experiencing extremes of heat; there is also nowhere to go, in terms of language, beyond 'boiling'. For these reasons, I have chosen the more moderate term 'global heating'.

'**Net zero carbon**' means reaching a balance between the amount of greenhouse gases we produce and the amount removed from the atmosphere. This involves reducing the amount of these greenhouse gases by 95% (to around 5% of current levels), and then compensating for the remaining emissions, for example by planting trees. More on this in Chapter 2.

Notes

1 Net zero carbon describes reaching a balance between the quantity of greenhouse gases we add to the atmosphere with the amount removed – by plants, methods such as carbon capture, etc. The 2030 commitment excludes the Church of England's investments.

2 Compounding an annual reduction of 26% gives a total reduction of 45% after two years, 59% after three years, and 95% after ten years.

3 'Report of the Church Buildings Review Group', 2015. The Church of England has some 15,700 church buildings, which roughly divide equally between the three grades of listed plus the unlisted – there are approximately 4,300 church buildings listed grade I, 4,300 grade II*, 3,700 grade II, and 3,400 unlisted.

Part I
Principles

1
Why Bother? Sustainability, Theology and Mission

Sustainability

If something is 'sustainable' it simply means it is able to endure. The way we use this word now in connection with the environment is the result of us finally waking up to the very real possibility that the choices we have collectively made put our very survival in question. While this book is specifically about the sustainability of church buildings, it is important at the outset to place this in the context of sustainability more generally.

In one general definition that speaks of its breadth and complexity, sustainability is described as:

> the integration of environmental health, social equity and economic vitality in order to create thriving, healthy, diverse and resilient communities for this generation and generations to come. The practice of sustainability recognizes how these issues are interconnected and requires a systems approach and an acknowledgement of complexity.[1]

There is much to like from a Church perspective in this definition. We too, through our mission and ministry, are engaged in creating 'thriving, healthy, diverse and resilient communities for this generation and generations to come' – God is interested in human flourishing, and this is what a community-oriented life lived in obedience to God looks like. And note those key words related to the practice of sustainability – interconnectedness, systems approach, and complexity; all of these will feature later.

In 1987 the landmark UN Brundtland Commission defined sustainable development as 'development that meets the needs of the present without compromising the ability of future generations to meet their own needs'.[2] This again speaks of balance, and a concern with the interests of communities at all levels (from parish to global) through time – moving beyond our narrow focus on this present generation's short-term interests. Definitions such as these suggest that sustainability is an arena where the Church should readily be able to engage – we know about the nurturing of community, and with our self-description as the communion of saints we already think in terms of community through time.

Christianity and the Environment

Way back in 1967, the American historian Lynn White published a much-referenced article, 'The Historical Roots of Our Ecologic Crisis'.[3] White places responsibility for the ecological crisis firmly at Christianity's door; he sees its anthropocentrism – placing humanity at the centre – as responsible for the crisis, accusing Christianity of an arrogance towards nature. By contrast, White sees St Francis as offering a more positive model, indeed as 'a patron saint for ecologists', for his proposed alternative view of the relation of humanity to the created order.

White's article has been attacked for its oversimplification, particularly in its treatment of Scripture. Nevertheless, his criticism endures. It does so because modern science and technology grow from an understanding of the natural world as a resource at the disposal of humanity, as opposed to something with which we are intimately connected, and because (for the most part) Christianity has emphasized the separation of humanity from the rest of creation. Certainly, many in the scientific community have now adopted something like White's view of Christianity's culpability; whether the argument is justified or not, it has stuck, and the Church can expect to be challenged increasingly forcefully in these terms as we engage with those around us.

Christianity's reputation is not helped in this by the funda-mentalist approach that draws on an overly literal reading of the Book of Revelation to argue that if the natural world will be replaced by a new heaven and a new earth, then it doesn't matter how much of the current created order we destroy. But this is just bad theology based on an impoverished reading of Scripture. Surely, God is not in the business of destroying the creation he so lovingly made, but rather in redeeming it; the Incarnation stands as God's vote of confidence in the created order.

A Little (Eco-)Theology ...

For Christians, how we see the environment says a lot about our theology. The charge of the harm caused by Christianity's anthropocentrism opens the question of how humanity should relate to the natural world – and this is very much a theo-logical question. As mentioned in the Introduction, alongside the responsibility of questioning our theological assumptions in response to the climate crisis, there is also the opportunity to expand and enrich theology to include not only the relation-ship of God to humankind, but to the whole of creation also.

It may be that theology is not your thing – though I would argue that all Christians are theologians because we all need to talk about and to God, and that if we don't do the work of shaping our own theology then we will be dictated to by the theology of others. Or maybe you are very much into theology, in which case you may find some of the authors referenced in this book more to your liking than others. The main take-away is that good people are doing urgent theological work, reflecting on how humans should relate to the rest of creation. Collectively, and to varying degrees, these authors challenge the worldview we have inherited which places humanity at the centre, and which ends up reducing creation to a resource at our disposal.

In her book *Biblical Prophets and Contemporary Environmental Ethics*,[4] Hilary Marlow explores what an ecological reading of

Scripture can contribute to contemporary environmental ethics, rooting her argument in a detailed textual study of Amos, Hosea and the first part of Isaiah. She extends the triangular relationship between God, Israel and the land into a 'creation triangle' or 'ecological triangle' comprising God, humanity and non-human creation, as the basis for a theological environmental ethics.[5] The key here is the *interrelatedness* of the three parts, and the impossibility of separating humanity from the rest of the created order. To read Scripture with this triangle in mind, and with a focus on those interrelationships rather than the division between humanity and nature, reveals markedly different insights, and challenges the anthropocentrism that Lynn White and others have so criticized.

The recent book *Green Theology*, by Dutch theologian Trees van Montfoort,[6] offers a wide-ranging, international and ecumenical exploration of this three-way relationship. Books such as this help demonstrate that sustainability is essential to any healthy theology – not a bolted-on application of theology, but a desperately needed corrective to our generally lopsided theological understanding of humanity's place in God's world.

... and Some Mission

Just as sustainability represents a massive opportunity for theology, so too for the mission of the Church. The international Anglican Communion has Five Marks of Mission, of which the Fifth is 'to strive to safeguard the integrity of creation and sustain and renew the life of the earth'. Interestingly, this Fifth Mark was added in 1990, six years after the original four were formulated, in response to the growing understanding of the missional and biblical implications of the climate crisis. That's more than three decades ago – what have we all been doing ...?

Where the Church is able to provide leadership on this issue, sustainability can have a powerful missional effect, not least because the younger the demographic in our society, the more the issue of environmental responsibility speaks. This, of course, is the inverse of the demographic of many churches. How great would it be for Christians to be known for our integrity on this issue, and to open up dialogue with increasingly unreached sectors of society?

Sustainability is an issue that opens up conversations with people who will otherwise have no contact with a living church community, embracing this issue will take us out into the world in new ways of collaborative working. Again, this is a fundamental of sustainability – if we are to stand any chance of avoiding the desecration of God's beautiful creation that humanity is causing, with all the suffering that will entail, then *we have to work together* – there simply is no other way. Scary, yes, but exciting also. Those denominations that have adopted the ambitious 2030 net zero carbon target have provided individual churches and other denominations with a strong lead.[7] And central to this is the clear framing of sustainability in terms of the mission of the Church.

And Buildings?

For many church communities, part of their response to the environmental crisis will include looking for ways to improve the sustainability of their church buildings – and it is to help address this need that this book has been written. Many church buildings are, of course, historic and listed, but that does not mean that they cannot be altered. The general cultural change we witness around us has also (believe it or not) reached into the cloistered worlds of heritage and conservation. Now it is common to see solar panels on listed buildings, including some of the most protected grade I buildings. (Or, rather, they may be there, but you are unlikely actually to see them – that's another story that we will return to in Chapter 4.) What was unthinkable 15 years ago is becoming much more widely accepted. This is another important way in which our culture is changing with respect to sustainability, and for the Church to take a sustainability lead – locally, regionally, nationally – is a huge opportunity to reach out into our communities. We have a once-in-a-generation (if not century) opportunity to reshape the Church's relationship with our culture; our buildings – including some of the most historic ones – will be an important part of that story.

Once we begin contemplating alterations to our buildings, it is important to understand a bit about how building projects work. Embarking on a building project is not like buying a new piece of clothing or a new car – the process is more complex and multi-dimensional, and more creative too. How a project is organized will have a big impact on the outcome; to succeed, five things need to be in place, five proverbial ducks in a row. These can be summarized by the acronym 'STAMP' – *Spirit* (zeal, passion), people with *Time*, good technical and professional *Advice*, *Money* (which will be attracted to a compelling story), and *Permission* (which may involve responding to opposition). All five of these 'ducks' need to be in place for a project to succeed. This book cannot help you with the *Time* and *Money* – you will need to find these for yourselves, perhaps with outside help. It primarily addresses the third of the five (*Advice*), but it hopefully also encourages the first (*Spirit*) and gives guidance on achieving the last (*Permission*), particularly where your church building is listed.

Sustainability presents the Church with an opportunity to extend our community, and to demonstrate our commitment to the common good. When working with a church building, it is important to see beyond its functional role of accommodating the activity of the church community. Instead, the relationship between community and building is more intimate – the community animates the building, and in turn the building itself helps to shape the community and give it identity. The relationship between a community and its building is therefore less one of master and tool, and more like two partners in a dance, just like humanity's relationship with the material world more generally, as discussed above.

Notes

1 UCLA, 'What is Sustainability?' See Resources R1.
2 See Resources R1.
3 See Resources R1.
4 See Resources R2.
5 Richard Bauckham uses a similar model in his *Bible and Ecology* – see Resources R2.
6 See Resources R2.
7 The Methodist Church adopted the same 2030 target, described as 'aspirational'.

2
General Principles

Before we consider specific alterations we might make to our church building to improve its sustainability, it is important to discuss some general principles. Let's start with the difference between carbon emissions and energy use.

Net Zero Carbon and Energy Efficiency

The focus of most climate commitments, including by the Church of England General Synod, is carbon reduction. Given that climate change is our greatest challenge, and that this is being driven by the carbon emissions from human activity, this is wholly appropriate; but it is not the same thing as energy reduction. The environmental impact of our activities is a combination of where our energy comes from, and how efficiently we use that energy. For example, if I were to heat my house using 100% renewable electricity while leaving all the windows open, that would have a very low carbon footprint, but it would be very wasteful of energy (not to mention being very expensive).

The point is that we need to address *both* our carbon footprint *and* our energy use/waste. The current focus is (rightly) on carbon reduction. But we also need to acknowledge that the root of the crisis we now face lies in having taken energy for granted for so long. We have enjoyed decades during which energy has been plentiful and cheap, and we have not had to worry about how much of it we use – hence, historically, lots of houses that were built with single glazing, poor airtightness and no insulation. Alongside a focus on carbon reduction, we also need to learn to use energy much more efficiently.

Four General Principles for Working with Church Buildings

While church buildings vary hugely in design, construction and use, there *are* some general principles that should be discussed before we consider specific forms of technology. The first principle is to *do your maintenance well*. I know, boring, isn't it! But this is relevant for various reasons. First, doing maintenance to your building is a bit like brushing your teeth – it is a basic life skill, a habit we hopefully acquire early in life which avoids a lot of physical and financial pain later on. Similarly, normal, everyday building maintenance – things like clearing gutters, making sure drains are taking rainwater away from your building properly, decoration of woodwork, etc. – prevents the financial pain of more expensive repairs later.

The sustainability relevance of maintenance is that avoiding your building becoming damp also reduces fuel use and avoids wasting money on your heating. Because water conducts heat well, a damp building uses more energy to reach a given temperature than a dry one. And even at the same temperature, a damp building will *feel* colder than a dry one, because damp surfaces around us absorb more of the radiant heat from our bodies than dry ones do, while dry surfaces reflect more heat back to us.

Please note that 'damp' is a relative term – what we are talking about here is *unnecessary* dampness, for example from blocked rainwater goods causing water to stream down the walls. And, to state the obvious, the climate crisis means that the climate is changing, bringing with it more extremes of rainfall. That means that even a properly maintained rainwater system of gutters, downpipes and drains that has worked well for generations may need to be overhauled or replaced to increase its capacity, to avoid being overwhelmed in our new climate reality.

This first principle of environmental design prioritizes 'fabric first', meaning that one should address deficiencies in the basic structure – walls, floor and roof – of the building before adding in clever technology. Typically, this means improving thermal

11

insulation and airtightness; in historic listed buildings, while there *may* be opportunities for both of these, 'fabric first' means attending to basic repair and maintenance before contemplating clever technology.

A second general principle is to *use electricity instead of fossil fuels for heating*. The reason for this is the ongoing decarbonization of the electricity supply – see the 'Two Greatest Commandments' section below. In terms of how heat is delivered to the users of the building, this typically means either through direct conversion of electricity to radiant heat (particularly relevant for less busy buildings) or using electricity to extract ambient heat from the environment through air or ground source heat pumps (for busier buildings only).

Related to this, a third general principle is that *the pattern of use of the building determines what alterations should be considered*. Underfloor heating is a great solution for a tall space without airtightness (like many churches), but only if that space is used regularly through the week. Without that pattern of frequent use, underfloor heating will be very expensive to run, because lots of energy is put into heating up the floor, which is given back to the space over the hours and days that follow with no benefit. So, if the space is only used for occasional, isolated events, this will be hugely inefficient and expensive. Similarly, solar panels on the roof may be an excellent complement to the other systems in the building if it is occupied enough to make use of the power generated; if not, they will still contribute to the greater good, but would achieve little benefit for the congregation itself.

A fourth general principle is that, while we may refer to a church as 'the house of God' (and mean different things by that), *what is good for the homes we live in won't necessarily be good for our church buildings*. Of course it's a natural thing to expect the latter to be like the former, because our houses are the buildings we know best, and this is something that we have been doing for centuries. But it can be really unhelpful. More on this below in the section 'Thermal Comfort'.

The upshot of all the above is to say: 'It's complicated!' And it is complicated because we need to think more broadly than we're used to, including factoring in not only the particular nature of the building itself, but also how people use it. And the decisions we take – for example when installing heating – will have an impact potentially for several decades to come; so planning change to our church buildings involves betting on how the building will be used in future. This is another example of how sustainability requires us to think holistically.

The Two Greatest Commandments are These ...

Having argued that it's complicated, let's try to make it simple. When it comes to carbon reduction, there are two basic principles. Paralleling the discussion between Jesus and the lawyer in Matthew 22.38–40, we could call these the 'two greatest commandments':

> The greatest and first commandment is this: 'Move from fossil fuels to electricity for your heating.' And a second is like it: 'Use the electricity you use well.' On these two commandments hang all the law and the prophets.

It is worth unpacking these two 'commandments', as what follows – particularly the discussion of specific technologies in Chapter 4 – does indeed flow from them. Let's take each 'commandment' by turn.

The first 'commandment' is all about the fact that where our power comes from is changing, and in a good way. The reason we should switch to electricity as our heating source is that the power network is progressively decarbonizing; that is, the proportion of electricity that comes from fossil fuels – coal and gas – is decreasing. Back in 1990, 77% of electricity was generated from fossil fuels, all of it coal; the remaining 23% came from nuclear.[1] By 2021, fossil fuels had reduced to around 40%, of which coal is now close to zero, with the remaining 60% a mix of renewables and nuclear. That year, in the lead up to the COP26 conference, the UK government committed to a goal of 2035 to decarbonize the electricity grid entirely. That remains an ambitious target; the Climate Change Committee's 2023 report 'Delivering a Reliable Decarbonised Power System' provides detail, and 25 recommendations, on how this can be achieved.[2]

At the local level, the implication of this decarbonizing of the grid is that we all need to move ourselves away from fossil fuels and towards electricity for the heating of our buildings. And we do not need to wait for the grid as a whole to decarbonize, because we can choose to buy our electricity on a 100% renewable tariff, reducing the carbon footprint of our energy use to zero. That, in turn, has the added benefit of encouraging further investment in renewables. (For a discussion of why hydrogen is almost certainly *not* the answer, see the section on 'Heating' in Chapter 4.)

The second 'commandment' – to use electricity well – has many different applications, which will vary according to context. For example, a heat pump is in line with this commandment, because it leverages every kWh consumed into roughly 3kWh of useful heat. So too with radiant heating, because it transmits the heat benefit of each kWh of energy used across an airspace to heat the solid surfaces it is pointing towards *without losing any energy along the way* – unlike a conventional radiator system which heats a lot of air, only a small proportion of which benefits people within the space. Heated pew cushions use electricity well, because they deliver heat (semi-)directly to our bodies via our backsides. Or again, better heating controls help us spend our precious units of energy more wisely.

Before anything else, there is the underlying maxim that we should do what we reasonably can to reduce our energy consumption. This points to a problem underlying the climate crisis as a whole – that in the twentieth century we all got used to cheap energy. Many campaigners would say we got hooked on the drug of cheap energy; our economies are now geared around it. Take car design, for example; it was only with the price hikes of the 1970s oil crisis that manufacturers seriously engaged with fuel efficiency, which rapidly moved from near irrelevance to become a prominent marketing feature. It is for the same reason that most of our buildings are hugely wasteful of energy, with insulation standards only being enforced later in the twentieth century, again from the 1970s onwards (and then only for new buildings). As a result of the choices we have made, when energy costs suddenly rise, as they did following Russia's 2022 invasion of Ukraine, large numbers of people are thrown into fuel poverty – that is, they cannot afford even basic heating. This can literally mean the choice between heating and eating – what an indictment of the way we have organized our society! One side-effect of the climate crisis is that we have (finally) been forced to think more seriously about our use of energy. The answer is not for government to make energy artificially cheaper, but to promote the transition to an economy that values energy more highly. That will mean revisiting old ideas such as encouraging onsite generation, refitting of thermally sub-standard buildings, etc.

Timing

If we are to address the climate crisis we need to take action sooner rather than later. This really is a crisis, and we need to act. Having said that, it is worth bearing in mind that for church buildings there are some key trigger points that will invite, or even demand, action. Perhaps the most obvious is when an ageing gas or oil boiler finally breaks down – as it may have been threatening to do for years – and we find it can no longer be repaired. That is a terrible time to start thinking about alternative heating solutions. I would like to see every church with a boiler having a plan for its replacement – it should really be a requirement.

Paraphrasing the Chinese proverb about when to plant a tree (25 years ago or, failing that, now), the right time to plan your replacement heating system is three years ago; the next best time is now. Boilers typically fail during cold weather; when they do, the easiest and quickest solution is to replace like for like. Then, once you have just put in a new boiler there will be little appetite to rip that out in favour of an electric-source solution. Much better to consider your options *before* you reach the crisis of the boiler breaking down, and then you will be ready when the situation arises. If you do find yourself unexpectedly without heating, the suite of Church of England heating guidance documents includes one on temporary heating options.[3]

But there are also particular opportunities for change. For example, where a church has radiators fed from a boiler, some of those radiators may stand attached to a bank of fixed pews, particularly in wider church buildings. Any reordering scheme will ask questions of how heat should be delivered to those in the space. Where fixed pews are retained, under-pew heating may be appropriate, but where some or all of the pews are to be taken out, a different means of heat delivery will be needed. It is also important to understand the strengths and weaknesses of your particular building, for which the latest quinquennial report (and the inspecting architect/surveyor who produced it) should be your first port of call.

It can be helpful to think in terms of three different modes by which we might engage with sustainability improvement. Borrowing language from customer services, when thinking of our church boiler (for example), we might be reactive (only considering sustainability when the boiler breaks), proactive (planning sustainability measures for when the boiler does break), or pre-emptive (proactively moving away from fossil fuel use in order to become more sustainable; before we're forced to). Clearly, the reactive approach is the least sensible ... but sadly also the most common!

Standards and Long-Term Thinking

Passivhaus is becoming increasingly well known as a brand for net-zero-carbon design; it refers to a design process, and from that a scheme of certification. In recent years, the approach has broadened from a focus on new buildings only to include EnerPHit, a related standard for retrofitting existing buildings, where the existing architecture and conservation issues render the Passivhaus standard inappropriate. Passivhaus is wonderful in its way, but it is only one solution, and it has some very specific requirements. As a process, it relies on high levels of airtightness, thick insulation, high-performance windows, mechanical ventilation with efficient heat recovery, etc. Most of these criteria will not be achievable for the majority of existing church buildings. As always, we need to be very careful about how we apply processes and technologies to existing buildings, particularly historic ones. To take Passivhaus as a template for making a historic church building more sustainable would likely be disastrous, because it cuts across the grain of what a historic building is and how it works. This is another example of the 'church is not a house' principle discussed earlier in the chapter. There are much better ways of making a historic building more sustainable, as outlined in the next chapter.

Again, a holistic view is essential, starting from acknowledging that historic buildings have always been very low carbon. Buildings built before the Industrial Revolution were, by definition, sustainable. In their construction and use, they made zero use of fossil fuels, instead using human and animal power, and locally grown timber (biomass) for the processing of building materials and their transport. Aside from the highest-status examples such as cathedrals or country houses, since transport was expensive, historic buildings were generally built using local materials; all of which, incidentally, contributes to the local distinctiveness of vernacular buildings, which we now so value. The materials used were typically very low carbon – stone dug from the ground by hand, timber grown and processed locally, etc. Brick production was more energy intensive, but then lime

– that ubiquitous material used for mortars, plastering, solid subfloors, etc. – is carbon-negative, consuming more carbon in its curing than it takes to produce. Lime is also much preferable for mortar in masonry walls, as it allows the brick or stone to be reused where cement mortar rarely does.

Contrast that with the energy required for the production of most modern building materials and components. This is referred to as embodied carbon – that is, the carbon emitted during the construction of a building. This is notoriously difficult to measure, but work is ongoing to develop an agreed methodology for historic buildings. Nevertheless, the principle is clear, that before we change any building or build anything new, we should consider the carbon cost of the building work and materials. One example is the siting of photovoltaic panels – if they are poorly sited in terms of orientation or shading, the carbon saving from the energy generated by the panels during their expected lifetime may well be less than the carbon cost and energy consumed in their manufacture, transport to site, installation and eventual disposal.

Thermal Comfort

Except for many of the busiest of buildings, a cultural shift is needed away from heating the entire air space and towards heating the people, particularly in less used buildings. Collectively, we have taken our understanding of what is normal in our centrally heated houses – that we should heat the entire air space – and have applied it to churches. Not only have we transferred that understanding, we have also transferred the same technologies – in previous generations we put central heating systems into our churches, generally comprising a gas or oil boiler that heats water to feed radiators around the edges of the space, with additional radiators attached to the front and back of fixed banks of pews where appropriate.

But church buildings differ significantly from our homes. Unless you happen to live in a baronial hall, the rooms in your home will likely have ceilings lower than 3m (10ft) – and often more like 2.4m (8ft). That means that the volume of air space is relatively modest (and most of it accessible to the people in the space), and heating the air makes more sense. Churches, on the other hand, are very tall spaces, typically upwards of 8m. This has several implications. First, the volume of air that needs heating is many times greater. Second, hot air rises – who knew?! – so tall spaces can often be all toasty at roof level while people are still shivering at ground level. This effect is known as 'stratification', and is something we generally never experience at home, because most of us don't live in very tall spaces. And third, churches are typically the opposite of airtight, with heated air constantly 'leaking out' through leaded windows, uninsulated roof structures with multiple gaps, poorly fitting doors, etc.

Instead of thinking about heating the space, we should be thinking about the thermal comfort of the people. Heating systems for homes, offices, schools, etc., tend to be designed to be comfortable over long periods of use and for people wearing light clothing – a typical design temperature might be 19°C to 21°C or even higher, and would allow occupants to wander round in shirtsleeves, shorts, etc. In most churches there is no need to provide that sort of comfort, or therefore those sorts of temperatures, because people are coming for shorter periods, and perhaps with an expectation that they will keep their jumpers and coats on while they are there. If this is the pattern of use of your building, to heat it to typical domestic levels would be both wholly unnecessary and very wasteful (remember the second 'commandment' above). It is important when rethinking your church heating to get some professional input (rather than relying on an installer, who is less likely to think in these terms). It's important, too, that the M&E engineer you work with understands how you use your building, and is willing to step away from the formulaic application of standard codes (some, sadly, don't and can't – more on working with professionals in Chapter 5). It may also be worth experimenting, by easing back on the heating until you get complaints – you may find that you are using your heating more than you need.

Comfort, of course, is affected by expectation, so before thinking about specific heating technologies, there is a more general discussion to be had around what expectations to design for, and these will vary from place to place and situation to situation. While many churches are used infrequently – that is, an hour on a Sunday morning – others are open and used from dawn to dusk, seven days a week. A church that is heavily used will have a quite different set of requirements for its heating system. Which is to say that the wide range of expectations of what levels of comfort are acceptable will be rooted in our varying understanding of what a church building is and our expectations of how we can use it.

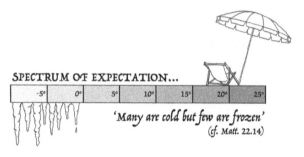

SPECTRUM OF EXPECTATION...

| -5° | 0° | 5° | 10° | 15° | 20° | 25° |

'Many are cold but few are frozen'
(cf. Matt. 22.14)

When it comes to comfort, we can think of a spectrum of expectation. At one end of the spectrum there is the view that church buildings need not and should not be heated to the same levels as our homes; instead, building users should adapt their behaviour to the building, for example by wearing more layers in winter. Perhaps at this end of the spectrum we're saying: 'Welcome to church, here is your snowsuit.' At the other end of the spectrum is the view that people are more important than the building, which should adapt to the expectations of its users. This latter view is often fuelled by a concern for mission – the Church exists precisely to engage with people who are not familiar with church, and draw them into faith; it follows that we must not let a cold building turn people away. This is not a debate that will ever be settled; instead we should recognize there is a spectrum of justifiable views, reflect on where we are on that spectrum, and perhaps explore other parts of the spectrum, for example by deliberately challenging our expectations.

Funding

Addressing the sustainability issues of existing buildings can often be expensive; while funding is not a principle, it is an ever-present question that deserves comment. In this context, it is very encouraging that the Church of England has set aside some significant funding to help with the move to net zero carbon. In the three years 2023–5, £30m has been committed to help this process – this covers not just churches but other buildings such as vicarages, church schools, offices, theological colleges, etc. The aim in those first three years is to support demonstrator projects, which in turn it is hoped will stimulate interest and raise ambition more broadly. That first £30m will be followed by a total of £160m over the following six years, by which time it is hoped there will be many more fundable projects. Clearly, that Church of England money is denomination-specific, and it's unclear what help will be forthcoming from central government, but it is to be hoped that this commitment will lead to the release of other funding streams.

That commitment was made (and this book written) against the political backdrop of a financial squeeze – the 'cost of living crisis' – in response to which in late 2023 the government relaxed the deadlines for its principal sustainability commitments. Whatever one's political persuasion, that was unwelcome from a sustainability standpoint, because the more we delay, the harder – and the more painful – the task will have become by the time you read this. All of which is a reminder that in a democratic system the political weather can always change, and that the Church should be praying for wise and strong leadership – including on sustainability – whichever party is in power.

The optimistic view is that the government will once again become ambitious and active in its support of the transition to net zero. Since the scaling back and cancellation of the renewables Feed-in Tariffs scheme, and the ending of the Renewable Heat Incentive, there has been a dearth of direct governmental financial support of the kind that would be so useful for church communities wanting to do the right thing. Moving forward, we should look out, for example, for new forms of tax breaks and grants to help make the transition affordable. Also keep an eye on the charitable grant bodies, as we can expect them to orient their programmes more towards sustainability; while this will never come close to addressing the need, such grants can be a means of leveraging other funding. The Church of England has a helpful guidance page on 'Fundraising for Net Zero Carbon and the Environment'.[4]

The cold reality, however, is that we cannot count on adequate external support for churches, because the public, denominational and other funding available will always be outstripped by the need. We are squeezed between two forms of affordability – we absolutely cannot *afford* (financially and morally) to ignore the transition to net zero carbon, but at the same time we need to find a plan that we can *afford* financially. Some churches will be successful in attracting substantial grant funding to transition their buildings to net-zero-carbon status, and we should celebrate these successes loudly. Many other churches will need to think smarter about how their buildings are used – for example, perhaps by using them less during the coldest months, or heating them less, or not heating all of them – and designing any interventions accordingly.

Principles that Apply to Almost any Building Project[5]

When embarking on a building project, there are some questions you as a church should discuss with your professional advisers:

- Consider the whole-life carbon of the project. Along with any carbon savings in the running of the building, also consider the carbon cost of the energy required to carry out the project, and the energy embodied in the materials and in their eventual removal at end of life.

- Carry out an options appraisal – including the option of doing nothing. Environmentally, which option will be best? For a small project, this might be a quick back-of-the-envelope exercise; for a large project, it might be fully costed options (including the carbon impact).
- Consider how long the work will last before it is changed or removed, and what would be required for it to last longer. Whether you are installing a kitchen, WC, floor, or heating system, the longer the work lasts the more sustainable it will likely be, and this should be weighed alongside initial financial costs.
- Consider how to minimize waste from the project, through reuse or adaptation in preference to demolition; plan for recycling of materials that cannot be reused.
- Link proposals to a broader sustainability strategy for the building through reference to the Practical Path to Net Zero Carbon (PPNZC – see Chapter 3).
- And don't forget the heritage significance of the building: under the permissions process for works to historic buildings, the benefits of any proposed changes must be balanced against their impact on the significance of the building (see Chapter 6).

Notes

1 All figures are from the Climate Change Committee – see Resources R1.

2 See Resources R1.

3 See Chapter 4 and Resources R4.

4 See Resources R4.

5 These principles are drawn from the EASA/CBC's 'Sustainability and Net Zero Carbon' Best Practice Note for Church Projects – see Chapter 5 for more discussion, and Resources R11.

3
Developing a Plan

Before looking at individual technologies you might apply to your church building, it is important to develop an overall plan. As has already been said, sustainability is all about taking the holistic view, not just focusing on a single aspect of the problem. It also considers shared wellbeing, not merely immediate self-interest – joined-up thinking is the order of the day. Thinking about your building holistically is a good thing in its own right, and it will also improve your chances of permissions success – more on this in Chapter 6. This chapter looks at two tools church communities can use to work on improving sustainability – Eco Church, and the Practical Path to Net Zero Carbon – as well as the usefulness of collecting data.

Eco Church

Many churches in England and Wales will already be familiar with Eco Church, which is an award scheme set up by the Christian environmental charity A Rocha UK for churches 'who want to demonstrate that the gospel is good news for God's earth'. For those in Scotland and Northern Ireland, the equivalent is Eco-Congregation. The Eco Church scheme involves completing a detailed questionnaire, which considers five areas of church life:

- Worship and teaching.
- Management of church buildings.
- Management of church land.
- Community and global engagement.
- Lifestyle.

The questionnaire comprises around 100 questions; the most detailed sections are the second: church buildings, and fourth: community and global engagement. The breadth of scope is a particular strength of the scheme – and very much in line with the holistic nature of sustainability thinking.

Completing the Eco Church questionnaire is best done by a group rather than an individual, not least because no single person will likely have access to all the information needed; it can also be really helpful to talk to a nearby church that has done it already. Once registered, the overall task can be divided between multiple people, for example with a different person taking each of the five sections. But more than that, the format encourages discussion and the measuring of progress. The scheme makes awards at bronze, silver and gold levels – as you complete the questions you gain points towards the levels. Once you have reached at least bronze across all five categories, you have achieved a bronze award. Then, having completed one level, it's almost impossible not to start looking at how to reach the next. Just reading through the questionnaire will prompt you in all sorts of ways. For example, you'll be challenged as to how much the environment features in your church's preaching, or in your children's work. How engaged on environmental issues is your church with those in your broader community? Or to what extent does the church challenge its members in terms of lifestyle issues?

Eco Church (and, outside of England and Wales, Eco-Congregation) is thus a fantastic way for a church community to raise awareness of what can be done to become more environmentally responsible, and to help build consensus. In effect it models a framework for what a church community that takes sustainability seriously looks like. However, when it comes to buildings, Eco Church would be the first to admit that its questionnaire does not form a plan of action – church buildings are hugely varied, as we have said, and the questionnaire does not begin to engage with issues of historic buildings. For that, something more specific like the Practical Path to Net Zero Carbon is needed.

Eco Church also has a comprehensive set of resource sheets

dealing with topics under each of the five main headings above, with additional material for children and young people divided by age group: 4–7, 7–11, 11–14 and 14–18. A subset of these resources is also offered in Welsh translation. Eco Church also publishes a magazine, *Root and Branch*, with some thoughtful articles. If you are committed to exploring how sustainability relates to Christian faith, Eco Church in particular, and A Rocha UK more generally, is the obvious place to go.

The Practical Path to Net Zero Carbon (PPNZC)

When we begin to think about individual changes we might make to a church building, some will be appropriate everywhere – for example, good maintenance and replacing older lamps with LED – while others will be more specific to your location (rural, suburban or urban), or to the age of your building (medieval to modern), or to its designation status (listing grade, local interest, unlisted), and indeed to how much the building is used. In the face of such variety, how on earth can one hope to provide any sort of general guidance?

The Church of England's Practical Path to Net Zero Carbon seeks to address this reality by offering a tiered structure of measures for consideration, starting from simple actions that nearly all churches can benefit from and moving to more complex interventions appropriate to more heavily used buildings. The PPNZC was the brainchild of Catherine Ross, the Church of England's Open and Sustainable Churches Officer from 2019 to 2023, and is aimed at church communities who want to make a contribution to addressing climate change issues, but do not know where to start.

The Practical Path builds on the findings of an energy audit programme covering Church of England church buildings that has been running since 2019. The resulting graph of energy use follows a logarithmic line, with a relatively small number of churches with high levels of energy use, and a long tail of churches with very low consumption. Clearly, for the Church as a whole to have the most impact on its carbon footprint, it

A practical path to net zero carbon
A checklist for your church

Our collective approach to net zero is underpinned by six principles:

Well maintained   Buy renewable   Waste less

Electric not gas/oil   Generate more   Offset the rest

THE CHURCH
OF ENGLAND
Environment Programme

is those churches with the greatest energy consumption – generally those that are most used – that should be addressed first.

Because church buildings come in all shapes and sizes and because they vary significantly in intensity of use, quite different measures are called for in different places. The Practical Path document succeeds in addressing a wide variety of such situations. The beauty of its graded structure is that it allows churches to start with the first tier of 'A' items, and over time to progress through the list, selecting those actions that are appropriate. Clearly a short document can never hope to be the last word; rather, its role is to encourage churches to make a start, and then to provide a framework for an ongoing discussion.

The beauty of the PPNZC format is that:

- it directs attention towards the most achievable improvements;

- it is responsive to the enormous diversity of church buildings;
- it encourages a holistic approach.

It provides a key tool for developing an overall sustainability plan and (if you can forgive the occasional bit of Anglican terminology) is applicable to churches of all denominations.

The Practical Path Structure

The Practical Path document packs a great deal into a small space – in its basic form, it's just two sides of A4. Being written for an Anglican audience, the document starts by pointing out that many of the suggested items require permission. This will also apply to listed buildings of other denominations, under their respective Ecclesiastical Exemption schemes; those few listed churches outside the Exemption will need to apply to their local authority for listed building consent. The document also stresses the need to seek input from professional advisers and the Diocesan Advisory Committee before making changes.

The document grades a total of 50 suggested actions into the following categories:

A *Where do we start?* These are simple actions that nearly all churches can benefit from, whatever their intensity of use. They are relatively easy, have relatively fast payback, and include such simple things as basic maintenance of the building itself, fitting LED lamps, and switching to renewable sources of energy.

B *Where do we go next?* These actions are more aimed at churches with medium energy usage which are used more than once a week; perhaps half of churches should consider them. The actions typically cost more than in 'A' above, and/or require more time and thought; some require some specialist advice and/or installers. Examples include considering alterations such as insulation in existing roof voids, creating a draught lobby, and creating separately heatable smaller spaces, all where appropriate.

C *Getting to zero.* These are bigger, more complex, projects, which only busy churches with high energy use are likely to consider. While offering substantial reductions in energy use, they also require substantial work, and have both a longer payback and a greater carbon cost. These include further insulation of the fabric, new LED lighting systems, and installing photovoltaics, all where appropriate.

D *'Only if ...'* These are actions undertaken at specific times (such as part of a reordering) or in very specific circumstances, and typically require professional advice (and, in an Anglican context, DAC input). Examples include adding insulation during a reroofing project, changing heat source and installing electric vehicle charging points.

E *By exception.* Finally, the document does not stop at recommendations, but also lists a handful of frequently discussed actions which are generally *not* recommended, because of the risk of harm to historic fabric etc.

The basic two-page version of the Practical Path can be downloaded from the Church of England website.[1] An expanded self-audit checklist version is also available, offering a useful starting point for churches, and this is reproduced in the Appendix.[2]

Other Use(r)s of the Practical Path

While the Practical Path is written with church communities in mind, it is also useful for others. Inspecting architects, surveyors, etc. have an important role to play in advising church communities, not least through the quinquennial inspection (QI) process in the Anglican system and for historic buildings in most other denominations. The inclusion of the Practical Path as an annexe to QI reports was a key recommendation of the joint EASA/Church Buildings Council working group which produced two sustainability Best Practice Notes for church architects and surveyors – for more on these, see Chapter 5.

The Practical Path offers church architects an excellent tool to encourage their churches to engage with sustainability issues in a responsible manner, while avoiding harm to historic buildings. Equally, as church communities begin to make use of this document, it can be expected that they may initiate discussions on the basis of it, so both architects and churches should make sure they are familiar with its format and recommendations.

For Anglican churches, the 2022 amendments to the Faculty Jurisdiction Rules now require that applicants for both faculty and List B permissions must 'give due regard to' the PPNZC; the idea is that the church is able to demonstrate how their proposal fits within the broader context of their route to net zero carbon. This will mean that in time it will gain greater use within the Church of England; despite the occasional Anglican-specific language (DACs etc.), it is in principle applicable to churches of any denomination, and remains the best such tool available.

Net Zero Carbon Routemap

The 'Routemap to Net Zero Carbon by 2030' (to give it its full name) is, as the name suggests, the Church of England's plan for how to reach net zero carbon by 2030. Adopted in July 2022, this document has a wider focus than just churches, also covering diocesan buildings, cathedrals, church schools, theological colleges and clergy housing. But the Routemap contains lots of good information and ideas for those who want to explore these issues further, as well as providing a sense of the overall picture of progress towards net zero carbon.

Collect Your Data

If we are to be responsible in the way we alter our buildings to reduce our carbon footprint, we not only need effort, money, etc., we also need data to tell us how the building is working at present. This is because church buildings vary widely in construction and thermal performance, and just as widely in how they are used (see the section on 'Thermal Comfort' above). The data will then inform how we might design a different heating system, or indeed, whether there are options to use what we've already got more efficiently. Alongside the numerical data discussed below, it can also be helpful to record *comfort data* as well – that is, surveys to record how comfortable people feel at various times through the year and during different types of activity – this will help when you come to brief a services engineer (see Chapter 5).

Data may take different forms, and come from different sources. The place to start is with your utility bills – electricity and gas or oil. Church of England churches can use the Energy Footprint Tool, which was launched in 2020 to provide a simple and effective system for measuring your energy use; this is done through the Online Parish Returns System. The tool also offers some specific improvement actions to reduce your carbon emissions, and allows churches to track the impact of the different steps they take towards net zero. An additional benefit is the invaluable data the tool contributes to the Church of England centrally – joined-up thinking and a view of the big picture are essential if we are to address the hugely ambitious target of achieving net zero carbon by 2030.

Installing Sensors

But however useful data from utility bills is, it only reflects the energy inputs to the building, and the cost of these. The next level of data to capture is temperature and relative humidity; this level of information enables us to understand how the building is performing at present, and is really useful for a services engineer tasked with designing a new heating installation. There are now lots of systems available online (search for 'temperature humidity sensor') which provide a base station and three or four indoor sensors with an upload to allow you to track performance via a website. I have no experience of these, but such systems rely on the building having wifi, and the thick walls of traditional buildings may also present problems. However, at the time of writing my practice has just installed sensors into four church buildings. Importantly, these systems include sensors that can be placed outside, and where the building has no wifi it can work via a dongle with a SIM card.[3]

To be most useful for understanding the building, the minimum sensible installation for a church would be four sensors. Two of these would be internal (one somewhere around person height, one at high level) and two external, one on the north side and one on the south. The two internal ones enable you to understand how much stratification there is (when the air is much hotter at roof level than ground level), and the two external ones help understand how external conditions impact the interior. Beyond that, one or two more sensors internally would be very helpful.

Sensors, of course, can only monitor conditions in the locations in which they're placed, so placement needs to be done with care – if you have a professional adviser on board, get their help in agreeing sensor positions. For example, the air in a corner may be colder or more humid than another location just a few feet away. Imagine how much more difficult it would be to create a cake mix in a rectangular mixing bowl – the mix in those awkward corners will likely be drier than the rest. So too with the air within any building with corners, particularly where the sides of the 'mixing bowl' are actively adding moisture to the 'mix', as with many historic buildings. Externally, sensors need to be placed out of direct sunlight – for instance, on the south side, behind a parapet, if you have them. If your church has sensitive furnishings or fittings – such as a good pipe organ – another sensor there would be sensible.

At the time of writing, the rule-of-thumb cost for the systems we have installed is roughly £200 for four sensors, plus £100 for the base station, plus £100 a year for the web platform subscription, plus £100 for non-wifi connectivity if relevant. So, not cheap, but worth it to avoid much more expensive mistakes.

Planning for 2030

If we are to be serious about the commitment to reach net zero carbon by 2030, then we need to plan what we are going to do when. The task is huge; as with eating the proverbial elephant, the way to achieve any large task is to break it down into achievable actions, and address them systematically one by one. Having a plan or route map can also be a great encouragement, if we monitor (and celebrate) our progress against the stages set out.

So, in this case, the NZC 'elephant' can be divided into parts; those parts should be 'SMART' – specific, measurable, achievable, relevant, time-bound – and we should be clear about who is tasked with working on each part. Consider using a simple table with those 'SMART' aspects across the top, and the measures you are going to take down the side. If you commission a more formal report from an adviser, you could populate the table from the report, or indeed ask the author to present their report in that format.

(No elephants were harmed in the writing of this chapter ...)

Notes

1 See Resources R4.

2 The content is almost the same in both versions – the checklist has a fuller introduction, but omits section E.

3 We have been working with the lovely people at Cheribim – see Resources R8.

Part 2
Technologies

4
Specific Technologies

This chapter reviews the principal sustainability technologies that are available, commenting on how they fit with different types of buildings. The key point here is that one size most definitely does not fit all. What is appropriate in one building or situation will not be in another. And that depends on multiple factors, as discussed in Chapter 3. It depends on the age of the building – historic buildings work differently to modern ones. It depends on how much the building is used – a building used seven days a week is very different from one used only on Sunday mornings. And it depends on the condition of the building – sometimes the most sustainable thing to do is some simple repair and maintenance.

Before we look at individual technologies, it is important to consider how we think about technology. It is easy nowadays to think of technology as something we 'bolt onto' aspects of our lives – we buy the latest kitchen gadget, television, phone or car, and off we go. However, applying new technology to existing buildings, particularly historic buildings, requires more thought and research than simply choosing our favourite shiny new piece of equipment. We need to think through the system as a whole, how the fabric of the existing building and its other installations will combine with the new technology. As has been said repeatedly, sustainability demands holistic thinking – and that's a good thing. It's not quite as stark as Jesus' warning about new wine in old wineskins (Luke 5.37–39) – how stupid, both will be ruined, Jesus is saying – but there's definitely a parable lurking in there somewhere.

So, while this chapter will consider different technologies in turn, it is important not to fixate on any one of these as *the* answer. The one universal rule is that, before exploring any of these additional technologies, it is essential to manage the heating needs of your church, for example through dull things like managing damp and draughts; only then can you hope to refine the right question to which these technologies may (or may not) provide part of the answer.

When reading this chapter, please keep one eye on the Resources section at the back of the book, particularly for the Church of England's range of guidance in R5, and Historic England's in R7. Resource sections R8, R9 and R10 provide further links. With several of the technologies in this chapter you will find prompts in the section heading to look at other technologies that may have a bearing on the topic in question. Think of this chapter not so much as a list of items, but more as an interrelated network of topics.

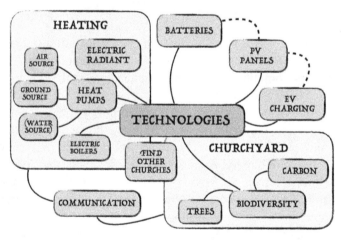

In all of this, it is important to get some appropriate in-person advice, from within your denomination and from your professional advisers. In the Anglican system, your first ports of call should be your diocesan environmental officer, net zero carbon officer, and DAC; in other denominations there may be similar people to help. If you do not already have professional advisers to turn to, this book will hopefully give you a head start and a frame of reference to help engage ones that will offer a good match for your needs – see especially Chapter 5.

Having considered individual technologies, the chapter concludes with a return to broader sustainability concerns with a short section on churchyards and biodiversity.

Heating

Heating accounts for some 80% or more of the energy use (and, if you are still using fossil fuels, the carbon footprint) of a typical church building. A heating system will affect the physical fabric of the building, its contents, the people who come to the building, and the church's mission.

Let's start by stating the obvious. Churches are often big buildings with high ceilings; they may only be used intermittently; and even when they are used there are not always large numbers of people present. All of which should affect how we try to heat them efficiently. Reflecting on this is what has pushed the Diocese of Bristol to experiment with radiant heating. As Simon Pugh-Jones says, 'We sensed that if we could only heat the bit we need, not the whole mass and volume, we could address that fundamental challenge head on. We did, it does, we have.'[1]

Because heating is such a central concern, the Church of England has developed a suite of guidance documents.[2] At the time of writing, these documents were as follows:

- 'Heating Principles'
- 'Heating Perspectives'
- 'Heating Approaches'
- 'Decarbonizing and the Future of Heat'
- 'Heating Checklist'
- 'Heating Pitfalls'
- 'Options Appraisals, and Getting Advice'
- 'Heating Permission and Regulations'
- 'Heating Costs and Funding'
- 'Temporary Heating Options'

You will also find examples of heat pump installations among the extensive range of Net Zero Carbon and Environmental case studies on the Church of England's website.

Why Hydrogen is (Probably) Not the Answer

There has been much talk of hydrogen boilers as a future technology that promises to solve all our problems. On the face of it, it's attractive, both because burning hydrogen produces no carbon at all – the only by-product is water – and because in principle we could simply swap out our existing fossil fuel boilers for hydrogen ones, without needing to replace the rest of our heating system. So what's not to like?

Unfortunately, there is increasing doubt about the usefulness of hydrogen (though for now the government is insisting that the research should continue) because of several difficulties. First, hydrogen corrodes the steel pipework used for natural gas distribution, which means in practice that a completely new infrastructure would need to be installed. Second, hydrogen is dangerous to store, because it is highly flammable – you may remember those iconic images of the Hindenburg airship disaster in May 1937. These factors mean that if hydrogen has its place as a fuel, it is in more contained industrial situations where greater security is possible, rather than as a widespread public utility.

Third, from a sustainability point of view, while there are almost limitless supplies of hydrogen in the environment (it is produced from water), hydrogen is very energy-intensive to produce. For hydrogen to be a green option, it would need to be produced using renewable energy. If, for example, we had significant excess capacity from wind power, then hydrogen production could use that excess power when conditions were windy. Even with the UK being so well placed to harvest wind energy, we are a very long way from having that sort of excess capacity, and a better use for any such excess would be to export it for use in nearby parts of Europe.

Finally, when you combine the various factors, the amount of energy used to produce hydrogen for heating is much greater than if you fed the energy direct to heat pumps. Professor David Cebon of Cambridge University compared the energy required to heat the UK's homes with hydrogen-powered hot water boilers and electric-powered heat pumps. Cebon demonstrates that the hydrogen solution doesn't just use a bit more energy – it would use 5.5 times as much![3]

In this context, the hydrogen conversation very much looks like a distraction and an excuse for inaction – putting off an expensive decision while waiting for a technical fix that never comes. Meanwhile, we are in the midst of a climate crisis that demands action *now*. For our purposes, hydrogen should be ignored.

And Why Hydrogenated Vegetable Oil (HVO) is Not the Answer Either

As above with hydrogen, HVO looks like a sustainable alternative to fossil fuels for oil boilers. However, there are significant concerns over supply chains and environmental credentials. A significant surge in demand has led to reports that HVO is being blended with palm oil, the cultivation of which leads to further global deforestation. Until demonstrated otherwise, HVO should join snake oil in the 'too good to be true' category.

Heat Pumps (see also PVs)

Compared with hydrogen-powered boilers, heat pumps offer a much better replacement for a fossil fuel boiler. Every electric fridge and freezer includes a heat pump, so they are hardly a new technology; the process is known as the refrigeration cycle (see following image). When applied to buildings, it is as though the fridge has been turned inside out: instead of absorbing heat from within the fridge cabinet and expelling it out into your kitchen via the metal grille at the back, heat is absorbed from outside and released inside the building via

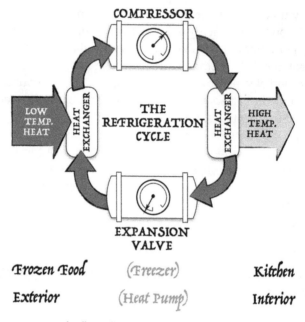

radiators or underfloor heating. And yes, even when it is cold outside, there is useful heat to be drawn from the air outside.

A heat pump works by compressing a gas, known as the refrigerant. Compressing a gas heats it up (think of a manual bicycle pump), allowing that heat to be used elsewhere (in our case, to heat our building). Once the refrigerant has delivered some of its heat into the building, it then cools as it is allowed to expand, making it ready to absorb more heat from outside and so to begin the process again. A heat pump consumes electricity, just as a fridge does, because it takes energy to run that process of compression and expansion. But in terms of usable output, a heat pump multiplies that energy input, typically by a factor of 3 or 4. This is known as the pump's Coefficient of Performance (CoP). A freestanding electric radiator directly converts energy to heat with no waste – it is therefore 100% efficient, and so its CoP would be 1. Instead of converting energy to heat, a heat pump *moves* heat from a heat source (external air/ground/water) to where the heat is required (within the building). Note that the CoP quoted for a heat pump will vary according to conditions, including the chosen output temperature. For air source heat pumps (ASHPs), efficiency does reduce as the air temperature reduces, but as a rule of thumb a CoP of 3.0 for an ASHP is a sensible average.

This feeds into the economics of heat pumps, for which the key measure is the relative cost per kWh of oil or gas versus electricity. For a considerable time, mains gas has been between a third and a quarter of the cost of electricity per kWh. Because of that average CoP of 3.0, when the cost of gas per kWh is a third of that for electricity, you would pay the same for the electricity to run an ASHP installation as you would pay for gas for a gas boiler. When gas is cheaper than a third of the cost of electricity per kWh (as it is at the time of writing), then it will be cheaper to run the gas boiler. That ratio will change. What it shows, however, is that you shouldn't think that a heat pump will necessarily reduce your running costs – the motivation needs to be longer-term and ethical rather than short-term and financial.

Oil, however, is generally more expensive than gas, so a different calculation applies. Prices have also fluctuated more widely, and are particularly susceptible to global political upheaval, of the sort we saw following the Russian invasion of Ukraine. Along with the relative cost of utilities, there are other variables in this calculation, including the CoP of the heat pump (which is gradually improving, but within limits), your scope for onsite generation (see the section on 'Photovoltaic Panels' below) and then for storage (see the section on 'Batteries'), and for cheaper night rates on your electricity tariff. The takeaway is that we should expect variation in the relative cost of utilities, and we should not expect a heat pump installation to be cheaper to run. While we should, of course, be mindful of costs, the prime motivation should be carbon reduction, not savings on running costs.

However, the CoP is not the whole story, because it is measured under standardized test conditions, much like the fuel consumption figures for a petrol or diesel car. By contrast, in reality a heat pump will have to perform under a range of conditions as temperatures vary through the seasons, so something more useful than the CoP is required in order to understand the likely real costs of running the heat pump over the course of a typical year. Enter the *Seasonal* Coefficient of Performance (SCoP) or Seasonal Performance Factor (SPF). This is something the heat pump installer is obliged to calculate, and is intended to show the likely efficiency of the heat pump through the course of a year, based on the specifics of your location and the heat delivery system to which the heat pump is connected. This, of course, is still based on average weather data, but will provide a much better predictor than the heat pump's CoP figure of projected running costs and efficiency.

Whatever the type, the heat pump will deliver heat via something internally, such as radiators or underfloor heating. The term 'radiator' here is potentially misleading, in that many radiators will give out more heat by convection (that is, by heating up the air) than by radiation, while underfloor heating emits substantially more of its heat by radiation. Another factor that affects the efficiency of a heat pump is the flow temperature of the water it produces; it works most efficiently if this flow temperature is limited to around 50°C. This compares with conventional oil or gas boilers which typically have flow temperatures of 80°C or more. That lower flow temperature means that the heat output we can expect from a given size of radiator is reduced, and therefore to maintain the same output when changing to a heat pump one needs also to change one's radiators for larger ones, or add additional ones. On the positive side, the lower flow temperature reduces the risk of children scalding themselves on very hot radiators or pipework, so one doesn't need bulky casings or cages around them to keep children safe.

Depending on the volume of water contained within the heat delivery system, a heat pump may also require a buffer vessel; this is very similar to a domestic hot water cylinder, and provides an additional volume of water to smooth out swings in heat demand, enabling the heat pump to operate more efficiently.

An alternative to delivering heat via water to radiators or underfloor heating is an air-based system – for example, pairing an air source heat pump with hot air blowers internally. This is very much like an air conditioning system, but for heating – though such systems can be specified also to produce cooling. The advantages of such a solution are that one doesn't need to upgrade existing radiators or indeed dig up the floor; it also has the advantage of quicker response times, and the warmth can be directed towards the people in the building. On the negative side, however, this solution still results in heating all the air within what is often an old, tall space that lacks airtightness, and there is also the issue that the wall-mounted heating units will generally look out of place on the walls of historic buildings, unless they can somehow be concealed.

Finally, one possible implication of switching from fossil fuels to electric heating may be a need to upgrade your electrical supply from single-phase to three-phase. Larger church buildings in particular may already have a three-phase supply, but there are many churches that do not. The type of supply you have is easy to tell from the number of 'tails' (supply cables coming into your meter) – if in doubt ask the electrician who does your five-yearly test and certification. The cost for upgrading to a three-phase supply can be substantial, and can only be determined by seeking a quotation from the electricity distribution network operator covering your area (for example, in South East England, the East of England and London this is UK Power Networks). This can be done by the services engineer who is designing your system (and yes, you do need a professional to design it).

Types of Heat Pump

We can divide heat pumps into three types by source – air source, ground source, and even water source – depending on where the ambient heat is drawn from. Air source is much the most common and often the most practical, ground source is possible, and water source is the exception.

The use of heat pumps to heat buildings is not new technology. London's Royal Festival Hall, built for the 1951 Festival of Britain, was originally heated with a water source system, drawing heat from the River Thames; the system could also be reversed and used to cool the building in summer. A few years before that, in 1945, John Sumner had installed a water source heat pump for the new Norwich City Council Electrical Department building. Almost a century earlier, in 1852, William Thomson (Lord Kelvin) had first proposed the use of heat pumps for space heating, and a ground source heat pump (GSHP) was patented in 1912.

So the technology goes a long way back. There are, however, some who have had bad experiences with heat pumps. This is usually due to either a badly designed system for the particular situation (meaning both the building and how it is used) or unrealistic expectations of how to use it. For example, when a heat pump is paired with underfloor heating it will not respond quickly when you return to a cold house after a nice sunny holiday.

Heat pumps are relatively expensive items to purchase, and need maintenance; this means that they will not make sense in a building that is in less-than-frequent use, like a 'Sunday-only' church. Let's look more closely at the practical implications for the first two of these three types of heat pump as applied to church buildings; see the 'Minority Technologies' section below for some more comments on water source heat pumps.

Air Source

An air source heat pump (ASHP) is a box with one or more large fans that sits outside and needs plentiful ventilation around it. Small 'monobloc' heat pumps are similar in function and appearance to the air conditioning units you might see hanging off the side of buildings in hotter climates; they might have a rating of around 5kW, and use a single-phase electrical supply. For a small church, a number of single-phase monobloc heat pumps may be adequate. Medium or larger buildings will need larger ASHP units which might be roughly 800mm deep by 2,000mm wide by 1,800mm high, with a rating of perhaps 35kW, and requiring a three-phase supply. As a very rough rule

*St Mary's, Ely: Two heat pump units within
a fenced enclosure.*

of thumb, one large unit like that might be enough to provide
heating for a small to medium parish church; a larger church
might need two (as installed at the grade I listed St Mary's, Ely).

Any ASHP will only function properly if there is good air flow
around the unit, otherwise it will be drawing in already cooled
air, and thus working inefficiently. It is important to understand
how air is brought into the unit, and where it is expelled from.
For example, a larger unit of the type described above will expel
the cooled air upwards – which means that any nearby vegetation might suffer. It is generally fine to put a fence around the
heat pumps, but if it is close to the unit it needs to be of hit-
and-miss design (that is, with generous gaps to allow a plentiful
supply of air through, as in the photograph of Ely above).

Siting of the units needs care generally, to ensure there is adequate space for maintenance. There may also be concerns over
noise impacting your neighbours. Again, it is true that ASHPs
can be noisy, but this is normally only when the machine senses
it is frosting up and it runs the fans faster to clear this, and generally the concern is overstated. Whether an ASHP is appropriate

will depend on there being an appropriate location, bearing in mind the proximity of neighbours (particularly domestic ones), and any heritage concerns (listed building, conservation area, etc.). Because an ASHP is an external change to the building, it requires planning permission (as well as any church permissions) – see Chapter 6.

Ground Source

The other main heat pump option is ground source. Even at a depth of around 1m, the soil temperature remains fairly constant at between 8°C and 12°C; this stability of temperature is a significant advantage of ground source, because the ground is significantly warmer than the air when you most need to heat your building. While air source will work at any air temperature we can expect ground source to work better when the air is coldest. This is reflected in a higher Coefficient of Performance of around 4.0 – that is, for every 1kWh used, the system can be expected to deliver 4kWh heat into the building. Ground source also does not have the noise issues, or the longer-term maintenance needs, associated with the fans of air source units. The disadvantages relate to getting the system installed – both higher capital cost, and disruption to the ground.

Ground source installations come in two quite different forms – horizontal trenches and vertical boreholes. The first involves digging trenches into which pipes are laid and then covered back over. These trenches are typically about 1.2m deep and wide (4ft in old money), and the pipework is laid in the bottom of the trench in horizontal loops; an alternative of narrower trenches at around twice the depth is sometimes used. Clearly this scale of excavation will not be appropriate in a historic churchyard where there will likely be lots of burials – remember that an absence of gravestones does not necessarily mean an absence of burials, since many historic churchyards have had headstones moved. But around a modern church where there are no burials, or where there is a car park that needs resurfacing anyway, etc., this can be a good solution. These pipes typically extract around 100W of heat per metre length of trench, so if you need to replace a boiler with 35kW output you would need around 350m length of trench; remember also that there needs to be 4m left between trenches.

Boreholes, on the other hand, do not disturb the surface in the same way, but instead go down to 100m depth or more, with the same idea as above of a sealed system that circulates a fluid that transfers heat from the ground to the heat pump. In principle, the further down one goes the better, because the ground gets warmer (geology dependent, but in the UK by an average of 2.6°C per 100m). However, the depth will be limited by the equipment and the geology. The boring equipment needs space to operate – but is small enough to come to site on a trailer pulled by a 4x4. Boreholes are potentially more appropriate for a churchyard, because each borehole disrupts only a very small horizontal area. However, the tops of the boreholes still need to be linked to one another and back to the pump, so there is some (narrow) trenching to be done as well. Where you have clear paths following old rights of way through a churchyard you are less likely (though never guaranteed not) to be disturbing burials, all of which means that a borehole solution could be viable, even in a historic churchyard.

Some rules of thumb: a 100m borehole might produce 3–4kW of energy, so a 35kW system would need around ten. Note too, that the boreholes need to be separated from one another by at least 6m, and preferably more like 8m, otherwise they will be competing against each other for the same ground heat. All of this – depth, output, distance – depends on the local geology. If you are serious about such a system, you would be well advised to commission a trial borehole, which will indicate how deep you can go and how much heat to expect each borehole to produce. Knowing the heat output needed then gives you the number of boreholes, and from there possible locations can be planned. In one local authority we were told that a single trial borehole would not require planning permission but that the others, once the array was designed, would. And in terms of cost, we understand this to be at least £10,000 per borehole (2024 prices), so only worth doing to confirm a favoured strategy. The trial borehole isn't wasted – it can be incorporated as part of the eventual array.

The heat pump itself would be the same whether you have a horizontal pipe array or a borehole system. It is like an oversized domestic appliance that is generally installed inside the building; it makes no significant noise, and would typically be located in a large cupboard or small store room.

Electric Boilers

An electric boiler directly heats water using electricity passing through a heating element, much like an electric immersion heater in a domestic hot water tank. If heat pumps can be compared to fridges (see above), electric boilers are more like electric kettles. Compared with a gas or oil boiler, they are not burning anything, so there is no flue to worry about, nor concerns with carbon monoxide or other harmful gases. There are significant advantages: they produce no onsite pollutants, so if you buy fully renewable electricity they are net zero carbon; they require minimal maintenance; and they do not require you to rethink your heat delivery (radiators etc.).

The big disadvantage of an electric boiler is that, because the electricity is used to heat water directly rather than to move heat from outside to inside (as with a heat pump), its Coefficient of Performance can never be more than 1.0, or 100% efficiency. That makes it three times as expensive to run as a typical air source heat pump, or indeed an existing gas boiler (assuming gas remains around a third the cost per kWh).

As an easy way of moving from a fossil fuel boiler, electric boilers have a place, but you should definitely quantify what your running costs will be. In general, there are other electric-source solutions that will likely be a better fit for your building, whether you need heating only occasionally, or use it intensively. But there are situations in which an electric boiler might be a good solution – for example, where heat pumps are not an option but where the building has access to cheaper electricity through plentiful PV panels.

At a much smaller scale, one common and very sensible application for this technology is the point-of-use electric water heaters used where small amounts of hot water are needed intermittently (for example, for hand washing in WCs) – the installation cost is relatively low, and the alternative of bringing hot water from a central storage tank would be inefficient (and thus expensive).

The takeaway is that electric boilers will only offer a good solution for general heating in a small number of situations.

Electric Radiant Heating

Radiant heating can offer a good solution for many churches, particularly those that are used more intermittently. Rather than directly heating up the structure of the building (that is, underfloor heating) or the air space (for example, blowers, conventional hot water 'radiators'), a radiant heat source transmits heat across an airspace in the form of infrared radiation and warms whatever its rays strike. The heat we feel from the sun is radiant heat, as is the heat from a patio heater. Just as the sun will heat us up, together with the unshaded parts of the bench we're sitting on, the wall behind us, the ground around us, etc., so too a radiant heater will directly heat human bodies and the surfaces around us. And crucially, it does this *without heating the air in between*.

Many radiant heaters glow red – for example, an electrical filament in an old electric fire, or the element in an electric patio heater. The latter is usually a quartz heater, comprising a heating element enclosed in a quartz tube – which emits both radiant heat and visible (red) light. Consequently, we know they're on because of the glow. These types of heaters are often found mounted internally on church walls. Their advantages are that they're relatively cheap to install, they provide instant warmth, and none of that warmth is wasted heating up the large volume of air within the building; for that reason they satisfy the second 'commandment' discussed in Chapter 2.

Personally, however, I don't like the red glow. Also, the type of radiation given out by quartz heaters is 'mid infrared' which does a better job of heating our skin than the rest of our bodies because of its relatively shorter wavelength. A complaint with these heaters can, therefore, be that heads feel scorched while feet remain frozen. But there are other types of radiant heater that do not glow red, and instead of the 'mid infrared' they emit 'far infrared' radiation (FIR). This has a longer wavelength, meaning it does a better job of warming us from the inside – so more warmth and less feeling of being scorched. It is the FIR in sunlight that does most of the warming we feel when we sit in the sun (while it is the ultraviolet at the other end of the spectrum that gives us sunburn).

FIR heaters come in different physical forms. The most common are plain rectangular panels (which can be finished in any colour to fade into a background). As with any light or heat source, the further away it is placed from us, the less the effect it has. In mathematical terms, the effect is inversely proportional to the square of the distance – so if the panel is 6m away from us we will feel only a *quarter* (not a half) of the benefit compared to if it were 3m away. Church buildings can often be very tall, so hiding panels against the underside of a roof 10m away may not produce much benefit for those shivering below. But they might work well, for example, on the underside of a gallery, where the ceiling is much closer to the people.

If you look on the internet, you will find lots of these radiant panels for sale. These are generally intended for people's homes, which therefore means they will likely be mounted within touching distance – for example, against a wall where one might expect a conventional radiator. As a result, they operate at a temperature similar to a hot water radiator (say 80°C), thus limiting their heat output. Radiant heaters for larger spaces, where the heaters can be placed well out of normal reach (beyond say 3m from people), operate at significantly higher temperatures (more than 200°C). If a church complains that they tried radiant heaters and they didn't work well enough, the type and the distance may well be the issue.

Issues and Strategies

As discussed, a common complaint with overhead radiant heating is that people's heads get hot, while their feet remain cold – and those with less hair will feel that effect all the more sharply! Far infrared is better than mid infrared for this, but it is also good if radiant heat is coming from more than one direction. The options are from above us, around us, and below us:

Above: It may be possible to attach heaters at high level to walls, or perhaps under galleries where they exist, or indeed to roofs or ceilings (remembering that inverse square law mentioned above). Or there are options for pendant fittings that combine lights with radiant heaters. Some of these use the rectangular quartz type heaters (red glow), which look quite clunky, but there are also options now for more elegant pendant fittings that combine non-visible FIR heaters with LED lights. One product, the Halo, has been developed by Herschel, a specialist in infrared heating (and named after the British astronomer Sir William Herschel who discovered infrared radiation in 1800).[4] The advantage of any sort of pendant fitting, of course, is to bring the heat source closer to the people, compared with mounting it on the wall or ceiling.

Around: Unless your building is really quite small, putting radiant panels at low level around the walls, even if there were space, would do little to heat those in the middle – remember, radiant heat is all about line of sight, so as soon as someone else gets between me and the heater I lose the benefit from it. Where a church has fixed pews, panels can be applied to the back of one pew to warm those sitting immediately behind; these can be wired to be switched locally, pew by pew, so that only the heaters that are needed are used, another example of using energy efficiently.

Below: There are also electric options for underfloor heating. You may have enjoyed underfloor heating in a bathroom; if so, this is often done with electric heating mats under the tiles or other floor finish. This might be an option when you are removing a timber pew platform, and are able to install some form of insulated floor build-up. (Electric mats are not suitable in conjunction with a timber floor of joists and boards because of the risk of a stray nail damaging the heating element.) The point of this sort of arrangement is that it provides a secondary source of radiant heat to balance the overhead radiant. And it would allow the church to still have pews, either fixed (with defined fixing areas free of heating mat) or movable, or to have chairs or open areas.

Heating is a great example of how with historic buildings one issue can often impact on several others. What is called for, therefore, is balance – not just between where the heat is coming from, but also between other factors, including how the building is used. One danger with any form of heating, including radiant, is the effect it may have on the physical fabric of the building. If you install lovely overhead radiant heaters, and one of them happens to point towards a sensitive piece of joinery, or a pipe organ, then significant damage may result. Or again, any new heating solution (including underfloor if there is a change of material and/or level) will have at least some impact on the visual feel of a church space, and that impact needs to be weighed against the benefits, as is explored in more detail in Chapter 6.

Photovoltaic (PV) Panels (see also EV Charging, Batteries)

Before getting into the detail of solar panels, it is important to cover some basics to focus the discussion. First, to clarify, in this section we are talking about photovoltaic (PV) panels – this means panels that turn light (sunshine mostly, but also more diffuse ambient daylight) into electricity. We are not talking about solar thermal panels, which directly heat water from the sun's rays – that technology can still have a place for heating domestic hot water, but one that is not relevant for most church buildings, because churches do not generally use significant amounts of hot water.

A second point is that PV technology is developing rapidly, and as it does the market is improving. Even in the last few years the efficiency of panels has improved (that is, the energy that a given area can generate), and the cost of installation is greatly reduced from what it once was. The flip side of this commodification of the market is that when dealing with historic buildings we need to take extra care with the choice of installer, the means of fixing the panels, the routing of cables, etc.

Finally, a PV installation should never be seen as an end in itself, but should be seen as part of the mix of sustainability measures you adopt. PVs are a great example of how sustainability calls for holistic thinking. It is one thing to establish that your church building could in principle house panels, quite another to be able to make good use of the energy they generate. This section attempts to address all of these questions, and give you pointers to where you can find further advice.

As already discussed in the Introduction and Chapter 1, we are living in a time of cultural change in how we think of sustainability, and this is exciting! Even in the last few years, it has become more usual to see PV panels on historic buildings – certainly not universally, but there are enough examples for it to have become more normalized. The key issue is the degree of visibility of the panels (see below), with panels generally not being allowed on historic buildings where they are visible. That raises a question, though, since thinking sustainability through from a theological perspective may well frame PV panels as part of the Church's mission (see also Chapter 1). If so, such an installation can be seen not as a fashionable add-on, but as part of the very purpose of the building. In that case, why should they not be evident, indeed celebrated?

In 2023 planning and faculty permissions were granted for the installation of PV panels on the roof of King's College Chapel, Cambridge, one of the UK's most prominent historic buildings. For more on why this is such a significant project, see the case study at the end of Chapter 6.

The Technology

Photovoltaics do what they say on the tin: they convert daylight – the 'photo' bit – into electricity – the 'voltaic' bit. While panels can generate some electricity from general daylight, they produce much more from sunlight, so installations need to be planned to take account of shading from nearby trees or tall buildings.

The panels produce DC (direct current) electricity, which needs to be converted to AC (alternating current) in order to be useful within a building. This is done by means of an inverter – a box on the wall positioned somewhere in the link between the panels and your electricity meter. Note that inverters have a shorter lifespan (10–20 years) compared to the panels themselves which can last for decades with only a very gradual decrease in generating capacity – important to remember when assessing the finances of an installation.

There are three main formats in which photovoltaic panels are installed:

- Large panels attached to rails that sit above the existing roof finish and are fixed down in some way, either by direct fixing or sometimes (for flat roofs) to a frame that is weighted down – this 'bolt-on' solution is much the most common;
- Integrated, where a pitched roof finish (that is, slates) is removed and replaced by trays, into which the panels sit – because the panels sit flush with the adjacent roof finish, they are less obtrusive, so may be more visually acceptable in sensitive locations;
- Building Integrated PV modules, for example solar PV slates, where a small PV panel is integrated into the visible surface of a slate; this has less of a visual impact, but because the panels themselves are smaller than a normal PV panel, installation costs will be greater. That said, this may be your only option. See Chapter 6 for the discussion of All Saints, Mundesley.

These three formats go from greater to lesser visual impact, and lesser to greater cost for a given electrical output.

Some Rules of Thumb

What follows comes with a flashing health warning: there are no hard-and-fast rules, because local conditions will always, rightly, take precedence. So always check with your professional advisers and the local planning authority before taking any action. With that proviso, it is helpful to discuss some general rules of thumb, in order to frame our expectations.

It is hardly news that church buildings are often oriented on a west–east axis, and their roofs tend to be rectilinear in plan – this typically results in one or more nicely south-facing roofs that could in principle accommodate solar panels. So, shading issues aside (adjacent tall buildings, large trees, etc.), churches are, in principle, well suited to solar panels.

But what of your chances of getting permission? Again, it's hardly news that church buildings vary in their heritage significance from the very ordinary brick-built hall to the spectacular and extraordinary grade I building of international importance. Local authorities are, rightly, keen to encourage the installation of PV panels, and church buildings that lack the heritage factor clearly have one less potential constraint around which to navigate. Note that you will still need planning permission along with whatever church permission you need for listed buildings under the Ecclesiastical Exemption – for more, see Chapter 6.

A second factor is then the form of the building. How steep are the roofs? Is the roof surface in question (and thus any panels) screened from view by parapets at the eaves? Or on a larger building, perhaps one roof is screened by other roofs. While the ideal angle for PV panels in the UK is 35°–40°, they can still work well at lower pitches, for example at the 10° typical for lead-covered flat roofs. For historic buildings, the rule of thumb is that where panels are not visible when approaching the building on foot – for example on a low-pitched roof hidden behind a parapet – then they are more likely to be permissible, though long views also need to be considered. King's College Chapel (see Chapter 6) is one example of this. Note that the implication of this may be that it is easier to get permission for panels on a grade I listed medieval church with low-pitched lead roofs

behind parapets, than on a grade II listed Victorian church with steeper pitched roofs where the panels would be much more obvious. That said, we are increasingly seeing examples of the latter, such as at All Saints, Mundesley, discussed in Chapter 6.

Cemetery Road Baptist Church in Sheffield (listed grade II) recently installed photovoltaic panels on its main pitched roof; in that case, rather than bolting them on top of the existing roof covering, the panels were installed in an integrated solution where the panels sit in trays that take the place of the slates; in this way, the panels sit down within the slope of the roof, making the installation much less obtrusive. Visually, this is a great solution, but is easiest to do as part of a general reroofing, with the bonus that less slate will be required.

The PV panel guidance in Historic England's newly published Advice Note, 'Adapting Historic Buildings for Energy and Carbon Efficiency', suggests that panels should be mounted on non-principal roofs such as valley roofs, and flat and low-pitched roofs which are concealed – or even on subsidiary buildings – rather than on principal roof slopes.[5] It remains to be seen how the planning system applies this guidance in practice.

Cemetery Road Baptist Church, Sheffield
(photo: Tom Crooks)

How Much?

PV installations are described in terms of their kWp (kilowatt peak) rating. When it was first introduced in April 2010 the Feed-in Tariffs (FIT) scheme was designed by the government to stimulate the uptake of renewable and low-carbon electricity generation. The basic installation was 4kWp – that is, the peak amount the panels would produce at any one time would be 4kW – so in an hour, 4kWh. In practice, this translates into an annual figure of around 3,200–3,500 kWh, depending of course on the weather. This roughly equates to average household electricity consumption – provided heating is not electric. So the idea was that a 4kWp system would roughly contribute as much electricity to the grid over the course of a year as the house consumes, ignoring how it is heated.

Church roofs vary hugely, of course, but are often larger;

where installation is possible, a typical British church building should be able to accommodate a sizeable array of up to 10kWp or more. However, even if you can accommodate a large array, you will need to check that the local grid infrastructure has the capacity to take generation above 4kWp – your services engineer will help you to do this.

Some Practicalities

In practice, the key to the successful implementation of PV panels is to think through in advance how the new installation will interface with the existing construction. This has a number of aspects:

- Will the existing roof structure be strong enough for the new panels? A structural engineer may need to advise.
- What is the condition of the existing roof covering? It's important to resolve any foreseeable defects, otherwise the panels will all need to be stripped off to effect a repair.
- How are the panels to be fixed? There are lots of options, from the rails that sit above a tiled roof as on many domestic installations, to the recessed trays (as at Cemetery Road Baptist Church above). For lead roofs, it is possible to build raised, lead-covered mounting points to which rails can be fixed (as was done in the King's College example dealt with in Chapter 6), or where the roof is strong enough ballasted frames have sometimes been used to avoid any fixings through the lead. Note that this concern with fixing is as much about wind uplift – with potentially disastrous consequences – as anything else.
- Where will cables be run? It is really important to plan where the cables will pass from outside to inside, and from there get back to the electricity meter – see the 'Service Routes' section below.
- Where will the large, wall-mounted inverter go?
- Where would you install batteries in future? – see the following section.

It is essential that these things are thought through and agreed in advance in conjunction with your professional adviser. Capable as many installers are, you cannot expect them to have experience – or indeed any understanding – of historic buildings. So be careful who you choose.

Managing Expectations

Photovoltaics can be an important part of our response to climate change. But they are at best only part of the answer. While they can generate useful amounts of electricity, don't imagine that they will make you self-sufficient. This is for the very obvious reason that the times when the sun is doing most of its shining (daylight hours, summer, etc.) is the opposite of when we have most need of the electricity (dark evenings, winter, etc.). Batteries enable us to manage the daylight v darkness issue (see below), but there's no fix for the summer v winter one. The best way of thinking of this is in terms of reducing (not eliminating) the electricity we pay for from the grid, while contributing to the greater good by exporting excess green electricity, meaning that less gas is used nationally to feed the grid.

Batteries (see also PVs)

This section considers 'batteries' in the widest sense – read on! An early word of warning – as with many other technologies, much of what you read online is written with domestic installations in mind, and there are some important differences. Again, as with other technologies, you should get advice from someone who is not trying to sell you a system or product – yes, you will pay for professional advice, but that will be much cheaper than buying an inappropriate product for your situation.

In principle, battery storage of the electricity generated from photovoltaic panels should be a game changer – a battery would enable you to generate electricity during the day and then use it after dark when you need the lights on. At the time of writing (2024), batteries remain expensive but, like other technologies, they are developing rapidly, and costs are beginning to fall. However, current battery technologies come at a significant environmental cost – it is unclear if those costs will ever be justified through energy savings. (That said, some companies (such as Nissan) now take batteries from old electric cars and reuse them for house installations, giving them many years of further useful service.)

Technical Factors

There are several different battery technologies, each with different characteristics. These technologies vary in terms of energy density (how much energy can be stored in a given weight or volume of battery), in power density (the rate of power output by weight or volume), in lifespan, and in financial cost. Importantly, they also vary in environmental cost – many batteries use rare-earth metals such as lithium, nickel and cobalt which, in their production, use huge amounts of water and can cause loss of biodiversity and soil degradation. Finally, while all commercially available technologies are safe, some are safer than others.

In terms of the siting of batteries, there are various things to consider:

- Weight – batteries are heavy (very roughly 30kg per kWh capacity), so can only be fixed to a structurally robust wall/floor;
- Temperature – too warm an environment will shorten battery life; so loft spaces are not good, particularly for lead-acid and nickel-based batteries;
- Fire – because of potential fire risk, batteries should not be located on an escape route, or near boilers; you should also discuss this with your insurers;
- Theft – there is a growing issue with battery theft, given the value of some of the metals they contain; again, something to discuss with your insurers;

- Flooding – if you're thinking of installing in a basement, then make sure you check for flood risk – water and electricity don't mix well!

Typical capacities of batteries are in the range of 2–15kWh, but are often extendable to greater capacities. It is essential to understand how battery capacity relates to your normal levels of usage, and to design the system to suit your specific situation including, crucially, how much and when the building is used. Costs for battery storage can be £500–£1,000 per kWh capacity, so you need to do your sums to make sure storage is financially sensible.

Types of Battery Technology

The three principal technologies that are currently available are:

- Lithium-ion (Li-ion) – like the Tesla Powerwall®, for example – this is currently the most common type;
- Lead-acid – old technology that might be relevant if you need lots of capacity (because it's cheaper), but these batteries have a relatively short lifespan; they also need to be well ventilated, because they give off hydrogen and oxygen when charging;
- Lithium-ferrophosphate (LFP) – this is a variant of Li-ion, but is free of cobalt and nickel, so is less environmentally harmful. It has a better discharge rate, deals better with higher temperatures, and has better lifespan and better safety; on the downside, it has a somewhat lower energy density, which simply means that for a given capacity the box will be bigger.

There are also a couple of future battery technologies to watch. One is solid-state batteries; these have up to 2.5 times the energy density of Li-ion batteries, charge faster and present fewer safety concerns. The other is seawater batteries. These (currently at least) have lower energy density, but in overall environmental terms look much more attractive, because they're made with sodium-sulphur, which can be processed from seawater, thus coming at far lower overall environmental cost, both in manufacture and disposal. They also have longer lifespans.

So, like a lot else, it's complicated, and this is an area where it may well be better to wait a few years to see how the technology develops. Meanwhile, as part of installing PV panels, it makes sense to plan for where you might install battery storage in future.

Other Options for Your Excess Power

Aside from battery storage, there are other ways of using the power generated from photovoltaic panels. If you were a church that had a high demand for hot water during the day, then it is very straightforward to send excess electricity direct to an immersion heater attached to a hot water storage cylinder to provide hot water free of charge. This is done with a solar diverter, which can be supplied and installed for around £1,000. On the other hand, if you have that level of demand for hot water, then solar thermal panels may be preferable.

Alternatively, for buildings that have a heat pump feeding underfloor heating, excess electricity can be used to pre-heat the building – essentially relying on storing heat in the structure which is gradually released into the space, thus keeping the space warm. This is using the long lag typical of underfloor heating to your advantage. Note that this effect lasts at most a few days – don't imagine this will see you through winter!

The default use of excess power generated on site is to export it to the grid. While the standard export tariff is a measly few pence, from an overall environmental point of view this is still a good thing to do because by generating and sharing that electricity we are reducing our nation's carbon footprint, even if we don't have a use for that power on site.

Finally, if you're able to sign your church up for a tariff with a more generous export rate, then that may well change the financial calculation. Once again, professional advice is worth paying for, and a financial appraisal is essential.

Windows and Airtightness

If you were to build a new church, then you should use double-
or triple-glazing for the windows and make it as airtight as
possible, just like any other new building. Most churches, however, are existing buildings, with a good number of them listed
and very old. If your existing church is unlisted and modern,
then it may be worth replacing your glazing to improve the
insulation value and airtightness. In moderately sensitive historic
situations, secondary glazing (a second layer of framed glazing
inside each window reveal) may well be feasible, but this makes
opening windows for ventilation more complicated.

In more sensitive situations, such as a medieval parish church,
changes to the glazing are – currently at least – a non-starter.
And that's because there is general agreement that the impact
such changes would have on the character of the building is
not justified by the benefit that would result (for more on this
principle of the balance of harm and benefit, see Chapter 6).
However, depending on its condition, the existing glazing may
well be letting in a lot of draughts. Individual pieces of glass
can get broken by birds flying into them, or by stones (whether
thrown up by lawnmower or miscreant). Beware, however, of
blocking up a hole that has become an entry point for bats
– because bats are protected, this can have significant legal
consequences.

More generally, leaded glazing gradually slumps over time
(say 100+ years); as it does, gaps open up between the glass
and the individual lead bars (known as 'cames'). Airtightness
can often therefore be improved by re-leading the windows. It's
certainly not cheap, but it's a predictable maintenance requirement for many historic buildings and needs doing if your glass
is not to fall out.

A final and very obvious means of reducing draughts through
windows – and thus heat loss – is to ensure that any opening
vents can shut properly. Vents need a periodic overhaul – again,
this should be part of a basic maintenance regime. And historic
doors can also be very draughty – here, time-honoured solutions such as heavy curtains can sometimes work well.

These are all examples of how basic maintenance is closely aligned with good sustainability practice. Again, this is the appropriate application of a 'fabric first' approach to historic buildings, as discussed in Chapter 2.

Service Routes

No, we're not talking about liturgical processions!

Sadly, one of the most frequent means of damaging a historic building is through installing mechanical and electrical (M&E) services. In our houses, it is very normal for electricians and plumbers to drill holes through walls and floors to route new services, and for gaps to then be filled. The same approach cannot be taken in a historic building, and the concern is that those doing the installation may or may not have experience of working in more sensitive locations where more care is needed.

There are three strategies we can adopt to reduce the impact of M&E services installations. In the context of a historic building that is several hundred years old, services are often very transient, and the first strategy is *reversibility*. (There is a whole area of interest around the preservation of historic technolo-

IN SERVICES (ARE) WE TRUSSED

gies, but that is another story altogether.) Reversibility means considering (and if necessary detailing) every hole and fixing – for example, reducing the number of fixings, and where possible fixing into mortar joints, rather than directly into the brick or stonework etc. – all with a view to the eventual removal of services and equipment once they reach the end of their useful life.

The place to start in planning service routes is by making use of existing routes, where these exist. For example, many churches have trenches set into the floor (often created by the Victorians) for carrying heating pipes – this below-ground infra-structure can be an excellent way of getting new cabling and/or pipework from one end of the building to the other. Services often also add to the sense of visual clutter, with some buildings seemingly trussed up in cables and pipework. It's important, therefore, to look for appropriate ways of hiding them – for example, above a continuous ledge or 'string course', or at low level within a pew base void. Sometimes wireless controls can be used to avoid the need for physical connectivity. These are all examples of the second strategy of *mitigation*.

A third strategy is the *minimization* of interventions, for example by using the same route for more than one service, prioritizing the least disruptive routes over the shortest, and surface mounting of services, rather than chasing them into a wall, as is common in domestic situations. Historic England offers further helpful guidance.[6]

Electric Vehicle (EV) Charging (see also PVs)

Charging of electric vehicles (EVs) will be a possibility for some churches. Clearly, the first requirement is somewhere to park at least one car – if you have a church with no parking at all then skip this section. Again, the Church of England has a good initial guidance document.[7]

Why would you want to install electric vehicle chargers? First, they're useful for those visiting your building, particularly those who are visiting from a distance, as may be the case with

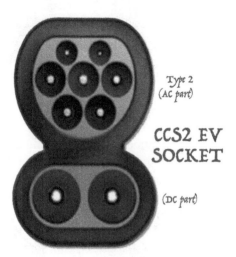

Type 2 (AC part)

CCS2 EV SOCKET

(DC part)

weddings, funerals, etc. The number of EVs on the road is increasing rapidly, so demand will only grow. Second, they are a tangible gesture of hospitality, as well as providing a demonstrable sign of a commitment to net zero carbon. Third, if you have PV panels on your building then an EV charger could be a good means of using excess electricity generated on site, particularly during summer months when you are generating most electricity but need less for heating and lighting. And fourth, EV charging potentially offers an income stream for the church.

Connectors

Do you remember there was a stage when there was more than one format for video players (Betamax, anyone?) before VHS became the standard? Similarly, there is more than one type of EV connector. The European standard is now 'Type 2', a 7-pin connector for AC charging at home and at public chargers up to 43kW. To complicate matters, on most cars this is combined with two extra pins at the bottom which allow higher speed DC charging; this is known as a CCS (Combined Charging Standard) connector.

The other connector type you might see is CHAdeMO, previously favoured by Asian manufacturers, and an alternative standard for DC charging. Some new cars such as the Nissan Leaf continue to use this format, but they will always also have a Type 2 socket for home AC charging.

The upshot is that for churches considering putting in EV chargers, Type 2 is the sensible option.

Charging Speed

Not all chargers are created equal! Depending on the type and weight of the vehicle, each kWh of electricity might take an electric vehicle, say, 3.5 miles.[8] Chargers installed at someone's home will usually be 7kW, and these are also common for general public chargers, such as at supermarkets – a car that averaged 3.5 miles per kWh and which was left to charge for two hours on a 7kW charger would add 49 (3.5 x 2 x 7) miles of range.

As chargers have increased in capacity, the terminology has become a bit confusing. In the UK we currently use the following terms:

- Slow – 2.3kW to 6kW (AC) – includes the direct three-pin plug option, and on-street lamp-post chargers;
- Fast – 7kW to 22kW (AC – single- or three-phase at 32A);
- Rapid – 43kW (AC) or 50kW (DC);
- Ultra-rapid – 100kW to 350kW (DC).

All rapid and ultra-rapid chargers have tethered cables; slow and fast may be tethered, or untethered, requiring the user to provide the cable. These different charging speeds are appropriate for, and therefore are found in, different situations – ultra-rapid and rapid typically on motorways and other major routes, and slow and fast in more local situations where the car may be left to charge during the working day, or overnight, or where it is used simply for a top up. The zapmap.com website is a good place to see what local provision is like, and therefore what need there might be.[9]

Installation and Set Up

'Rapid' and 'ultra-rapid' require much greater investment in infrastructure than is appropriate for a church, which will therefore usually be installing the 'fast' type. Where a church has a single-phase electricity supply (like most homes), that means one 7kW charger; if you have a three-phase supply, you could install more than one 7kW charger or a 22kW charger. Clearly you will need to think about the siting of your charging point(s), and how cables will be run from there back to your electricity meter.

In terms of permissions, you will likely need planning permission (but check with your local authority) to install a charger. Since 2022, within the Church of England system, requirements have been relaxed somewhat; for unlisted buildings, EV chargers are now classed as 'List A' – that is, they can be installed without a faculty and without the need for DAC consultation – while for listed church buildings, 'List B' permission is required. All such installations must meet a set of criteria – see Chapter 6 for more detail.

There are two basic means of installing an EV charger. Churches can host a charger or chargers installed by a third party, and then receive rent or a proportion of the income from the charger. Or they can fund the installation themselves and charge customers directly for usage. With the latter route, there may be some grant monies available via the Office for Zero Emission Vehicles – the government's interdepartmental team working to support the transition to electric vehicles.[10]

Finally, with the right type of charger, it is possible to allow different charging rates – for example for church staff, for church members and for the general public.

Minority Technologies

There are various other technologies which, while unlikely to be relevant in the great majority of cases, still deserve a mention.

Water Source Heat Pump

For this to be relevant, your church building would need to be close to a watercourse, lake, or substantial pond. The approvals required are more complex than for air source or ground source, because you would need permission from the Environment Agency – they will, rightly, be concerned about the impact of the installation on biodiversity, which can be affected by the chilling of the water. In principle, such a solution might perhaps work for an estate church – where a country house has, for example, an ornamental lake with sufficient flow through it – but I'm not aware of any examples at present.

Note that there are two options here – known, respectively, as 'closed loop' and 'open loop'. In a closed loop system, the heat pump cools a transfer fluid and circulates it through pipework, in this case submerged in water, which draws energy from the water; the liquid never makes direct contact with the body of water, it simply transfers the heat. One leading heat pump manufacturer, Kensa, markets what they term 'pond mats', comprising coils of pipe fixed to stainless steel frames which are sunk to the bottom of the pond or river.[11] Note that, to avoid the risk of freezing, the depth of the water is important – if the water is still then it needs to be at least 1.2m deep; if flowing, then it can be shallower. There is also a potential concern with mechanical damage from water traffic – no punting allowed!

With an open loop system, the water from the pond or stream is itself the medium of heat transfer – water is extracted from one location, passed through heat exchangers in the heat pump to absorb energy from the water, and then the cooled water is discharged back into the water source either downstream of, or at some distance from, the intake. Given the bigger scale and additional permissions required, such a system would be unlikely to be workable for an individual church. Interestingly though, it was water source heat pumps that were first installed in the UK, as at the Royal Festival Hall, as discussed above.

Bath Abbey offers another one-off. As part of their 2021 refurbishment, underfloor heating was installed throughout the church fed from the limitless supply of naturally occurring hot water from Bath's hot springs. So if you do happen to have a hot spring nearby, you might have a highly sustainable solution to your heating needs ...

Hydroelectricity Generation

While very few churches would have a watercourse running through the churchyard, there may be some in remote areas, or others where a project might be feasible as part of a community-wide initiative. The principle here is to pass water through a turbine and back into the watercourse – in much the same way as a traditional water mill is powered. In its favour, this is an efficient source of energy, and is endlessly renewable (provided your watercourse is not seasonal). It is also productive in winter, unlike solar panels. However, it requires expert engineering advice to design and install the system, and once again would require approval from the Environment Agency as well as planning permission.

Biomass

This refers to a type of boiler that uses organic material as fuel – for our purposes, this means burning wood (generally in chip or pellet form) – to heat a building. A biomass boiler would likely, therefore, be a replacement for a fossil fuel boiler. Like any gas or oil boiler, a biomass boiler releases carbon into the atmosphere; it is credible in terms of sustainability when wood is used that would otherwise simply rot – for example the unusable waste from wood production – and where this harvesting is accompanied by replanting. However, burning of wood also emits nitrous oxide, which affects the ozone layer, and particulates, which have a negative health effect. Together with the constant attention they need to keep them working, these factors mean that biomass boilers are not generally recommended. In practical terms, for such systems to be workable, much more space is needed than an equivalent oil or gas boiler. To work properly, you also need constant heat demand – for example a building that keeps its underfloor heating going all through the winter. You also need to be confident of a dependable and consistent supply of fuel, and suitable access for deliveries of that fuel. Storage of the pellets or chips takes a lot of space, and needs to be adjacent to the boiler, which requires a constant slow feed, generally by means of an auger.

Wind Power – Don't Even Think About It!

In the early days when architects began thinking about sustainability, it was fashionable to put a wind turbine on top of your new building. This was never a great idea; to generate a worthwhile amount of power, the turbine needs to be large, and it needs to be located in an exposed and windy location. Single wind turbines can work for farmers, particularly for off-grid locations without mains electrical supply, so if your church is remote and in a very exposed location, then this might be something worth looking at, but you'll be the exception that proves the rule.

The Zero Emission Boiler (ZEB®)

ZEB® is the trademark of a company called Tepeo. Their technology is very simple – they use electricity directly to heat a dense concrete core – very much like a centralized storage heater. For its efficiency (the 'second commandment' from Chapter 2), it relies on clever monitoring and the use of cheap night-time electricity, so you would need access to that sort of tariff. The ZEB® calculates when and how much to charge: it learns how much heat your building needs, it uses local weather forecasts to predict the energy needs for the day ahead, and is able to make adjustments throughout the day as needed. An app lets you adjust how the ZEB® should charge, and you can always boost the ZEB® manually – for example in advance of a special service.

This is a developing technology which is currently targeted at the domestic market; there are no known installations in churches, and it would only work for small buildings with relatively modest heating loads. The advantages are that a ZEB® is a direct replacement for a conventional boiler, so requires less additional change compared with many other technologies; it will also work with PV panels. The Tepeo ZEB® is a little bigger than a standard washing machine, but is very heavy (all that concrete in the core), so needs a solid base to stand on. The installed cost at the time of writing is something like £10,000, and the storage capacity around 35kWh.

As already indicated, this will only work in a small number of church situations at best. But the combination of simplicity, clever controls, the use of cheap nighttime electricity and ease of installation makes this a technology to watch.

Finding Other Churches

As part of the Church of England's Online Faculty System, there is an interactive map showing the use of renewable technologies.[12] This allows searching by diocese, by listing grade, and by technology, including ASHP, biomass, GSHP, solar PV panels, solar thermal panels, wind turbine, and EV charging. Thus, one could search for all examples of PV panels on grade I and II* listed churches within a selection of particular dioceses.

However, it has to be said that the information is less than complete, though there is a form for uploading missing information.[13] Imperfect as the data may be, it is nevertheless a good place to start when looking for churches that have successfully installed renewables, particularly photovoltaics or ground or air source heat pumps. It allows churches to prepare a shortlist of other churches to approach to learn from their experience – whether or not you are part of the Church of England.

With all of what I have termed these 'minority technologies' in the section above, there will be particular places where they can be the best answer. But the smaller the pool of installed examples, and thus of available expertise, the more important it is to learn from others who have experience of the technology, to be careful to seek external advice, and to reflect on whether it would work in the same way in your particular situation.

Water Use and Toilets

We tend to think of the UK as having more than enough rainfall, particularly when we see (or experience) flooding, which is becoming more frequent as the climate heats up. But with a combination of modern lifestyle expectations, population growth and hotter summers, we risk finding ourselves short of water more frequently. We should treat water as the valuable commodity that it is.

Church buildings are not generally large consumers of water – hence it usually makes financial sense to install a water meter – but there are always things we can usefully do. For example, we can consider replacing basin taps with ones operated by motion sensors – these are more costly to install because of the electrics, but they do save water and, with fewer moving parts, should be less likely to need repair. Simple push-down taps are a simpler alternative that will also save water, provided they cut off quickly. If you have a churchyard with tended graves, then having a water butt for visitors to water flowers is a simple means of reducing water consumption – just be sure the butt is installed with an overflow to a surface water drain, not just into the ground.

Global heating is causing heavier and more concentrated rainfall with implications for your building's whole system of rainwater goods – gutters, hoppers, downpipes, gulleys, etc. A system that was well sized a generation ago may no longer be adequate. This is worth thinking through with your inspecting architect, who should be able to advise.[14]

Toilets

In rural situations without mains drainage there are a couple of technologies that enable a toilet to be installed.[15] The first, the composting toilet, uses no water in its operation; over time, the waste is turned into compost that can be used as excellent fertilizer in the churchyard. If you're interested, make sure you talk to other churches who have them, to learn from their experience.

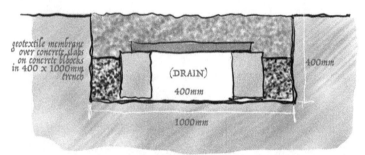

geotextile membrane over concrete slabs on concrete blocks in 400 x 1000mm trench

(DRAIN)

400mm

400mm

1000mm

TYPICAL TRENCH ARCH IN SECTION

The second technology is a conventional water-flush toilet connected to a 'trench arch drain'. This involves digging a long trench in the churchyard, which has a bare earth base, with concrete block sides and a concrete slab lid, which is then covered over with geotextile membrane and soil, and typically planted with grass again. The waste from the toilet discharges into the trench arch drain, where the fluids drain away into the earth and microbes and worms digest the solids. Clearly it is important not to kill the organisms in the drain with conventional bleach-based products, but we should be moving away from these anyway, wherever our drainage runs to. You will need a percolation test to determine the absorption rate of the soil, and permission from the Environment Agency – again, take professional advice.

Both of these solutions are more sustainable than our mains system, which relies on the industrial-scale processing of sewage, and which can get overwhelmed by concentrated heavy rain.

A septic tank may be a solution in some rural situations but, given the size of excavation needed, this is unlikely to work if your building is surrounded by burials.

Churchyards

This last section moves the focus back out from specific technologies to the broader ecological picture. It is important to see the church building and any churchyard as an integrated system. Churchyards are important for sustainability both for their biodiversity, and because they store carbon. Churchyards are one of the best illustrations of the principle that, with sustainability, everything relates to everything else. Caring for God's Acre (CfGA) is a well-established national charity that promotes the conservation of burial sites, including churchyards; they have a fantastic, freely downloadable Action Pack split into some 35 topics, including information on biodiversity and – importantly – how to involve others in your local community.[16]

Biodiversity

Churchyards are often ideal oases for wildlife: birds nest and feed in them, wildflowers thrive (if allowed to do so), and many churchyards have mature trees which may in their own right be host to a whole micro-environment, as well as being important features in the landscape or townscape. Grassed areas within churchyards can be particularly important for wildflowers, butterflies and insects – a churchyard can often be the only fragment of unimproved, wildlife-rich grassland for miles around. If so, it will be a sanctuary for particular species in your area, and perhaps also a staging post, providing a vital link with other sites as part of a network that allows species to move, spread and survive.

What you do in your churchyard will, of course, depend on your specific situation and location. There are many possibilities, including the following:

- Survey what species of plants and animals you already have in the churchyard and share this for everyone to see.
- Consider planting trees, but be careful of blocking important views of the building, or indeed shading it if you might install photovoltaic panels; remember that trees will also need regular inspection (see the next subsection for more on trees).
- Install bird boxes, bat boxes, wood piles, 'bug hotels', etc.
- Plant hedges where appropriate – they provide shelter and winter food for birds and animals.
- Consider where you could let ivy mature – it is great for pollinators such as bees and butterflies – but somewhere it won't cause damage to the main building(s), churchyard monuments, boundary walls, etc.
- Plant herbs, which are delightful for humans and also great for pollinators.
- Leave lichens and mosses on walls, headstones, etc. (note that some are protected species).

The main message is to be thoughtful about what you do. Take the time to understand what you've got, and take advice as necessary – if you have a county wildlife trust, that would be a great place to start.

Trees

Many churches have beautiful trees in their churchyards or grounds, sometimes several hundred years old. They form part of the character of the site, and along with hedges will always host a range of wildlife, as well as playing a useful role in absorbing carbon. It can therefore make sense to plant more trees and hedging, but this needs to be done with care. Existing trees and hedges may form an important part of a historic landscape, and any new planting needs to be properly considered from a landscape design perspective.

It is also important to consider the impact on the church building, and any other structures in the churchyard or near to it. Trees that are planted too close to an existing building can in time threaten its very future. It is also important to consider how a church building might need to be extended in the future – once the stem of the tree grows to 75mm in diameter it automatically becomes protected (in conservation areas and around listed buildings).

Communication

When it comes to churchyards, it is important not just to encourage biodiversity, but to build consensus with your community and to *explain* what you're doing.[17] For example, once we stop mowing our churchyard within an inch of its life, display material becomes key. Why? Because it is easy to look at a churchyard with longer grass and to interpret that as neglect, a lack of care, whereas the opposite is true! What short memories we have – we have forgotten the cultural change that came with the mass production of motorized lawnmowers from the 1920s onwards, which led us to think that short grass was normal in a churchyard. We're now going through another time of cultural change, which requires bringing people with us. Cutting a mown route through an area of longer grass is one way of achieving the benefit while still communicating care.

Managing your churchyard differently provides great opportunities for (re-)engagement with your community. Churchyard work parties can readily lead local people who otherwise have little contact with the church to volunteer. Work parties can also themselves be a ministry to those recently bereaved who want to care for the churchyard in which their loved one is buried.

Churchyards and Carbon[18]

Most of us are familiar with the importance of trees in capturing carbon – we should all be aware of the threat to the world's rain forests, and of the strategy of planting trees to offset our carbon emissions. Yes, trees are good at sequestering carbon, but shrubs, grassland, and the soil also do the same job. And remember that, in some circumstances, a badly placed tree can damage nearby habitats and lead to a net *release* of carbon – so, again, take advice.

Soil carbon, which enters the ground through decomposing plant matter, is much less understood than the role of trees in capturing carbon. When plant material dies and decomposes, some carbon dioxide is released into the atmosphere, but a great deal of the carbon and oxygen is directly incorporated into the soil. When bare soil erodes, previously stored carbon is released back into the atmosphere. But if left undisturbed, the soil will mature, with the top, 'active' layer – the part that is full of life and thus able to store more carbon – deepening. Undisturbed churchyards are especially carbon-rich. If you have areas of longer grass with wildflowers in your churchyard these should be cherished; compared with short mown grass, taller plants and wildflowers, because of their deeper roots, deepen this top layer of 'active soil', thus storing more carbon.

Notes

1 See link to 'Radiant Heating Trial, St Matthew's, Bristol' in Resources R5; also 'Halo Church Heating at St Matthew's', and 'Herschel Halo Heating: Performance Review', both in Resources R8. Simon Pugh-Jones is an architect and chair of Bristol DAC.

2 See Resources R4.

3 See Resources R1.

4 This is the type of fitting used at St Matthew's, Bristol; see 'Radiant Heating Trial' in Resources R5, etc.

5 Pages 30–1; see Resources R7. This document is relevant to a number of the technologies dealt with in this chapter, and to other possible sustainability-related alterations.

6 See Historic England Technical Guidance: 'Installing New Services' in Resources R7.

7 See Resources R5.

8 There are lots of variables that affect EV range, including air temperature, speed, driving style and, of course, how heavy and bulky the vehicle is.

9 They also have a helpful summary of charging speed terminology and connector types; see Resources R8.

10 See Resources R8.

11 See Resources R8.

12 See Resources R4.

13 Again, see Resources R4.

14 Changes to rainwater goods are also mentioned in Historic England Advice Note, 'Adapting Historic Buildings for Energy and Carbon Efficiency', page 34; see Resources R7.

15 See Resources R9.

16 See Resources R10. I personally have learned so much from CfGA, as reflected in the content of this section.

17 CfGA fact sheet D4, 'Telling the Story – Interpretation'. See Resources R10.

18 CfGA fact sheet A12, 'Improving the Carbon Footprint of Your Burial Ground'. See Resources R10.

Part 3
Processes

5
Working with Experts

Finding the Right Professionals

In addressing the carbon footprint of your church you will need to work with professional advisers. But how do you find the right professionals to work with? Start with your inspector (architect, surveyor, etc.) if you have one; all Anglican churches, and churches of other denominations with historic buildings, should have an appointed individual who inspects the building every five years (known as a 'quinquennial inspection' or QI). You can expect this professional to have a detailed knowledge of the condition of your building, its age and construction; they should also have at least a working knowledge of the relevant permissions system(s).

Of course, not all inspecting architects and surveyors are equally committed to addressing environmental concerns, so you may need to appoint a different architect for this work. If so, what should you look for? Clearly, alongside professional competence, they need to show sustainability literacy – at least a basic awareness of the issues. There is now some published sustainability best practice guidance for church architects and surveyors – discussed later in this chapter – which can give you a point of reference for assessing a potential appointee's approach. If your church is listed, then you should also probe for their approach to change in historic buildings, since this often accompanies sustainability improvements – I suggest you're looking for someone who is neither buccaneering nor preservationist. If forced to choose, the approach to change is perhaps the most important factor here, because it is a deep-seated cultural outlook which is unlikely to shift quickly; sustainability literacy, on the other hand, is a form of technical knowledge that can be learned.

Services Engineers

In order to reach net zero carbon, many churches will need to change either their building's heat source, or indeed the larger heating strategy. That requires design, for which you need a services or M&E engineer, who should not be confused with the gas engineer who services your boiler. A services engineer is an independent professional consultant who can assess your building and your needs, and design your new system appropriately. Look for someone who is a member of CIBSE (the Chartered Institution of Building Services Engineers). They should have the skills, knowledge and experience of the different types of technologies available; importantly, they should be independent from any suppliers/installers/contractors. Without that independence, the advice you receive will be skewed towards the particular technologies that person favours, whatever they might be. Hopefully, your architect will be able to recommend some good M&E engineers, and you can also approach your DAC or equivalent church body for a shortlist of possible names, but the appointment will be yours, and there are two issues I suggest you should consider.

The first issue is that it is very easy – and therefore common – for services engineers to over-design their systems, and this relates to specific technologies. The cost of over-specifying a fossil fuel boiler is negligible – often, the next model up in the range is only slightly more expensive, and efficiency is not at all closely related to the intensity at which the boiler is working. The easiest way for whoever specifies the boiler to avoid grief from an unhappy client is therefore to give them a boiler bigger than they really need. And when replacing a boiler – and it is now common to replace a boiler every 15 years – the default is to at least match the capacity of the previous one – so over the years this produces an inflationary effect of bigger boilers. By contrast, heat pumps are significantly more expensive pieces of kit which need to be more closely matched to required heat outputs. So you are looking for a services engineer who is willing to engage with what you *need*, not simply what is convenient to give you.

This brings us to the second, related issue for a services engineer: their understanding of comfort. Mechanical and electrical engineering is all about numbers, and services engineers use tables of design data – published by their professional body, CIBSE – to determine how much heat output is needed for a system. What is not usually discussed with clients are the assumptions about what is an acceptable level of comfort on which these tables are based. Comfort is highly subjective – different people experience it quite differently. Furthermore, rather than primarily being a scientific question with a measurable answer, comfort is more a cultural question shaped by our expectations. For example, if we expect to come into a church in the depths of winter and feel warm in shirtsleeves – as many people still do in their homes – that will require a whole lot more heat, and thus bigger and more costly equipment, than if we expect to keep coats and scarves on.

There are, of course, situations where a well-heated space is needed – for example, a toddlers group, or a sedentary activity for the elderly – but there are many other situations where we need to rethink expectations of how warm our spaces should be. The point is that to arrive at an environmentally responsive and responsible building you need a services engineer who is able to engage with this issue of comfort, look beyond the CIBSE standard tables, and give you advice tailored to your specific situation. This will require you as the client to communicate clearly your requirements and expectations for comfort. If you want a cooler building, you will need to deliberately instruct the services engineer that they should design for that; otherwise, they will (rightly) design to meet 'defensible norms'.

A Word to Conservation Professionals

(This section is a plea to conservation professionals such as church architects, who are key influencers in the care of church buildings, but churches may also find it relevant; if not, please skip to the next section.)

Architects, surveyors and other buildings professionals are

uniquely well positioned to encourage church congregations to embrace sustainability, and to promote change. For example, where an existing boiler requires replacement we can recommend an appropriate options appraisal. We can incorporate environmental issues into our QI reports. Where new rainwater goods are installed, we can anticipate increased future demand in a changing climate and specify accordingly. Much of this is existing good practice, and can all be achieved within the current framework for dealing with listed buildings under the Ecclesiastical Exemption.

We can also encourage parishes to rethink where they buy their energy from. Many churches still do not know that moving to a fully renewable electricity tariff is easy, or that the premiums for going green are tiny. With a few online clicks they could decarbonize *and* save money.

Whether we have an active Christian faith or not, as professionals involved in the conservation of churches we all have a longstanding *legal duty* under Section 35 of the 2018 Measure to 'have due regard to the role of a church as a local centre of worship and mission', to which in 2023 was added '… and the importance of environmental protection'. Since this is the way the mission of the Church is heading, church communities and their advisers all have a responsibility to engage wholeheartedly with this issue.

Responding to Change

As the world is waking up to the impacts of the climate crisis, we find ourselves in a rapidly changing landscape. If, as professionals, we think that conservation should itself be immune from change – or indeed that the Church's job is to shelter people from change – then we risk becoming part of the problem rather than the solution. We all have work to do! As professionals, we have to think through how to address sustainability without harming the significance of the buildings in our care. That involves some rethinking of the principles of conservation, and how we understand change to living historic buildings; we need to embrace change as a tradition-guided opportunity, and not merely as a threat to be avoided.

Change is central to the character of most of the historic buildings we love and care for. We measure history by reference to change – date built, date adapted, effect of fire, war, social change, etc. The carefully managed alteration of historic buildings in response to climate change can and should therefore be seen as heritage best practice – a legitimate cultural expression of the most pressing issue not just of our time but of the much longer lifespan of the buildings for which we care.

Sustainability does not mean thoughtlessly slapping new technology onto every historic building; but we should be bold in pushing against regulatory constraints on sensitive proposals where physical and visual impact can be minimized. We need to balance the established principle of minimal intervention against other increasingly urgent priorities; this is why, in a system that requires the balancing of benefit against harm, the framing of sustainability as an expression of mission is so powerful.

Sustainability Best Practice Guidance

The Ecclesiastical Architects and Surveyors Association (EASA) and the Church Buildings Council have jointly published two Best Practice Notes, one addressing project works, and the other quinquennial inspections; these are intended to encourage conservation professionals to address sustainability in their day-to-day practice. While written primarily for church architects and surveyors, it is hoped they will also prove useful for churches in understanding what they can expect from their professional advisers, and perhaps provide a framework for discussion. Both documents are available from the resources section of the EASA website.[1]

Launched in 2021, these documents were developed in response to the increasing public concern with the climate crisis and the many national, regional and local organizations that, in the preceding couple of years, had recognized the climate crisis and set targets for reaching net zero carbon. Most significant of these was the Church of England's adoption of its ambitious target of 2030, as touched on in the Introduction and Chapter 1 above. As a result, architects began to see church communities increasingly asking how they could improve the sustainability of their buildings, including their historic ones, and this will only continue to grow.

Both Best Practice Notes acknowledge that architects and surveyors are in a privileged position to encourage church communities in their ambition to be more environmentally sustainable – and, crucially, to achieve that ambition without compromising the heritage integrity of their buildings. The guidance provides a frame of reference for professional advisers first to spot appropriate opportunities for sustainability improvements, and second to offer guidance to churches. The aim informing the creation of both documents was to embed sustainability as part of the normal duties of these professionals – 'while you're there, comment on this' – rather than treating it as a separate or additional function or service.

Church Projects

The first document deals with project works; these come in a wide variety of forms, from significant re-orderings and extensions through to substantial programmes of repair. Such projects often present opportunities for improving sustainability; the Projects Best Practice Note offers a framework to ensure, first that such opportunities are not missed, and second that any proposal is well argued in the permissions process.

To that end, the argument for any sustainability measures should be integrated into the Statement of Needs, one of the two key documents on which permissions for change to historic buildings are determined. It helps to state explicitly some principles for sustainability proposals, touching on government and specific diocesan or equivalent policies, and (for Anglican churches) including reference to the Fifth Mark of Mission, as discussed in Chapter 1.

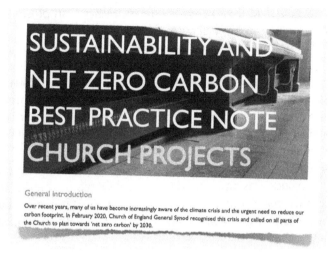

General Introduction

Over recent years, many of us have become increasingly aware of the climate crisis and the urgent need to reduce our carbon footprint. In February 2020, Church of England General Synod recognised this crisis and called on all parts of the Church to plan towards 'net zero carbon' by 2030.

The document starts with principles that apply to *any* project (see the end of Chapter 2 for an adaptation of this), before considering others that would apply to *specific types* of project, such as roof replacement, solar panels, re-orderings, etc. The renewal of heating systems is a very common type of intervention: changing from an oil or gas heat source to electric, combined with moving to a 100% renewable supply, typically offers a very substantial carbon saving. The Note makes reference to the Practical Path to Net Zero Carbon document discussed in Chapter 3, and to which applicants for Church of England faculty permission are now required to refer (see Chapter 6). The Note ends with recommendations on monitoring and data gathering, and a selection of useful links and resources.

Quinquennial Inspection (QI) Reports

The second document deals with QIs. Because they are carried out on a regular, five-yearly pattern, QIs present another key opportunity for inspecting architects and surveyors to support churches to reduce their carbon footprint. Again, the focus is on considering questions of sustainability during the normal course of the inspector's duties, rather than presenting a further, onerous layer of complexity.

Included in the QI Note are two sections of recommended standard text, one to introduce sustainability issues for inclusion in the preamble, and the other for a suggested 'Countdown to 2030' section, under which the inspector can then summarize their sustainability-related recommendations. It is important to remember that, at the time of writing, most churches will only have one more inspection before 2030.

Again, the QI Note refers to the PPNZC, recommending that this is included as an appendix to every QI report. Ideally, the church will have engaged with this in advance of the inspection to help prompt, guide and focus any discussion of sustainability issues.

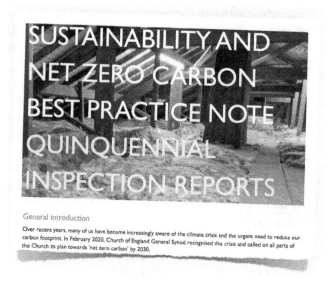

General introduction

Over recent years, many of us have become increasingly aware of the climate crisis and the urgent need to reduce our carbon footprint. In February 2020, Church of England General Synod recognised this crisis and called on all parts of the Church to plan towards 'net zero carbon' by 2030.

Extra Work?

Sustainability is all very well, but doesn't it all represent a lot more work for the professional? In one sense, yes, in that sustainability clearly represents another dimension to be considered in report writing and decision making. But mostly, no, in that this is a normal part of the process of the professions improving their knowledge base and skillset in response to changing client needs. As already stated, inspecting architects have a pivotal role to play in advising church communities. Rather than representing an onerous set of additional tasks, I suggest that engagement with sustainability should be embraced by professionals as a form of Continuing Professional Development, a valuable means of expanding our skills; once learned, such knowledge will improve the service we offer and should, in time, become second nature.

Where to Get Help

Within each Church of England diocese there should now be a diocesan environmental officer (DEO), and many now are appointing net zero carbon officers, or have additional environmental working groups or task groups. Other denominations may have similar figures in post. When discussing sustainability with a DEO or equivalent, it is very helpful to understand their personal background. Does their engagement with environmental issues begin from a concern with carbon reduction – which will likely mean they have experience of buildings issues – or are they starting from an interest in biodiversity? While it is of course possible to combine expertise in both, officers tend to approach sustainability from one or other background. The DAC (and equivalent Listed Buildings Advisory Committees in other denominations) will hopefully have members with a good degree of sustainability literacy that covers both areas of focus.

Note

1 See Resources R11.

6
Getting Permission

This chapter discusses some of the practicalities of the permissions process across the denominations; it has a particular focus on listed church buildings where, for obvious reasons, the greater challenges lie. Being listed does *not* mean a building cannot be changed, just that you will need to convince others that the benefits of any proposal outweigh any impact on the building's special interest – see the 'Responding to Change' subsection in Chapter 5, and the 'Arguing for Change' section below. But before getting into some of the specifics of getting permission for your proposed works, it's worth outlining the permissions framework that governs listed church buildings. If your building is not listed, then much of what follows will not apply – unless you're an Anglican church, in which case you will still need faculty permission, regardless.

The Ecclesiastical Exemption

The Ecclesiastical Exemption is a mechanism within planning law for listed Christian places of worship in active use to obtain listed building consent; it replaces the need to get this permission via your local planning authority for most listed churches. The Exemption is an administrative umbrella, a set of criteria within which individual Christian denominations develop their own systems to control alterations to listed church buildings. It is an exemption from listed building consent only, not from planning permission, nor from other permissions such as Building Regulations approval. To add complication, the Exemption applies in different forms in each of the four nations of the UK; in England, which has the greatest number of protected buildings, the Exemption covers five specific denominations – the Church of England, the Roman Catholic Church, the Methodist Church, the United Reformed Church, and churches within the Baptist Union.

Because of both the numbers and the highly listed nature of many Anglican church buildings, the Church of England's Faculty Jurisdiction is both the longest running and the most developed system under the Exemption, dating from well before the introduction of secular heritage protection in England. As a result, the system is legal in nature, and in each diocese is presided over by a judge, known as the 'chancellor'. While this can sound scary, it needn't be. On the positive side, it means that arguments are well considered, and where a decision is contested the chancellor's judgment will be written down and published. These judgments record the arguments in the case, and offer a set of precedents that may be useful; they also help satisfy the Exemption requirement for openness and transparency.

In 2010, the Department for Culture, Media and Sport (DCMS) published guidance to accompany the latest revision to the legislation.[1] This guidance requires that any procedures under the Exemption 'must be as stringent as the procedures required under the secular heritage protection system'; this 'equivalence of protection' is identified as a key principle, and one that will be kept under review to ensure that appropriate standards of protection are maintained (p. 7). There is always, therefore, the potential for the Exemption to be withdrawn, or indeed for a denomination itself to withdraw from it, as did the United Reformed Church in Wales in 2018.

The DCMS guidance appreciates the importance of keeping historic buildings in use, if they are to survive. It helpfully states:

The Ecclesiastical Exemption reduces burdens on the planning system while maintaining an appropriate level of protection and reflecting the particular need of listed buildings in use as places of worship to be able to adapt to changing needs over time to ensure their survival in their intended use. (p. 6)

This offers explicit recognition that, for living listed buildings such as churches, change is legitimate in principle, and essential to their survival as places of worship; at the same time, it points towards the brutal reality that, should the Exemption be withdrawn, the secular planning system would simply be unable to cope.

The nuts and bolts of how the Church of England system works are set out in the Faculty Jurisdiction Rules, which are periodically updated. The full permission process results in a 'faculty', but the Rules also contain two lists of works that do not require a faculty – List A describes works that require no consultation of any kind, while List B describes those that require sign off from the Archdeacon after they have sought DAC advice. Amendments were made to the Rules in July 2022 which explicitly sought to encourage engagement with sustainability. This update made obtaining permission easier for various sustainability-related changes, from simple improvements such as insulating pipes, draught-proofing doors and windows and fitting electric pew heaters, through to things like installing non-fossil fuel boilers and EV charging points. Meanwhile, moving in the other direction, the new Rules now require additional justification (and a full faculty) for replacing a fossil fuel boiler like for like, or for installing a new oil tank.

Other denominations and other nations of the UK deal with the approval of works to listed buildings under the Exemption in different ways. For example, some systems separate the advisory committee from the decision maker (as with the Anglican system), while for others it is the committee that also makes the decision (as with the Baptist Union). For any given church community, your first step should be to contact your denomination to understand how your system works and what information you will need to provide. My article 'The Ecclesiastical Exemption in Practice' provides an overview of the Exemption, if relevant.[2]

It is very important to understand that the Exemption does not excuse churches from engaging with secular heritage bodies, including Historic England (Cadw in Wales, Historic Environment Scotland, etc.) and others. At the time of publication,

Historic England had just issued an Advice Note on 'Adapting Historic Buildings for Energy and Carbon Efficiency'. This strikes a healthy balance between the acknowledged need to change and the protection of heritage. The first, highlighted paragraph is worth quoting in full:

> Our historic buildings must continue to change and evolve if they are to both contribute to a greener future and be fit for purpose for the people who live in, experience and care for them. If done thoughtfully and carefully, these changes can achieve the complementary goals of protecting our heritage and adapting to a changing climate. Historic England has produced this Advice Note to provide clarity on key considerations and to support consistent decision making.[3]

This framing of change as legitimate and necessary 'if done thoughtfully and carefully' – is important to hold onto. Change to historic buildings is natural – the issue is how we do it.

Relevance to Mission

Chapter 1 touched on the way sustainability is not only an *urgent* issue, it is also a profoundly *theological* one; this is recognized in the Anglican Communion's Fifth Mark of Mission, which is 'to strive to safeguard the integrity of creation, and sustain and renew the life of the earth'.

Whenever they were built, our church buildings were created to serve the mission of the Church – that is just as true for a medieval church as for a modern one. In an age in which climate change is for many the most pressing concern – the more so the younger the demographic – is it not reasonable for churches who see the promotion of sustainability as core to their mission to wish to make their commitment visible? Viewed as an integral expression of our mission, why shouldn't a church community seek to place photovoltaic panels visibly on their roof, for example?

Bristol was among the dioceses that pioneered a more responsive approach to sustainability and helped shape the ambitious 2030 net zero carbon target. Its DAC used this connection between sustainability and mission as a means to change the emphasis in their approach without having to re-write faculty legislation. Chancellors can include 'opportunity for mission' and the 'viability of a church as a place of mission' as among the key public benefits to balance against any harm to significance; those missional benefits clearly include sustainability.

Caring for the world is a vital and compelling issue, whether we see it in theological terms or not. Parishes embracing sustainability experience a galvanizing effect among their church family and find links strengthened with their wider communities. Sustainability is of strategic relevance within the broader culture, since local churches can act as a catalyst in their community for carbon reduction initiatives and climate resilience strategies. For the Church, both local and national, to be contributing to the national debate in this way is entirely welcome.

Specific Issues

Photovoltaic Panels

Significant external changes to existing buildings generally require planning permission. In some circumstances, installing photovoltaic panels is treated as 'permitted development' – this describes types of work that you can get on with without needing permission. For the most part these rights apply to domestic properties only, but they extend to some photovoltaic installations on other unlisted buildings, including churches.[4] The bigger challenge relates to listed buildings, where the level of control is, understandably, greater.

There is now a rule of thumb that, if your listed church with its lovely south-facing roofs can accommodate panels that won't be seen, then you are likely to be able to install them. So panels on a low-pitched lead roof behind a parapet are likely to be allowable, while more visible ones are less likely. See the case study at the end of this chapter for one prominent example.

As discussed in the previous section, the Fifth Mark of Mission (loosely, care for creation) is important for justifying change in an Anglican context, because it frames sustainability as a core part of the work of the Church. By treating it as part of our mission it is thus included within the public benefit that offsets 'harm' within the faculty system and other equivalent permissions processes.

Another interesting example that illustrates the mechanics of the decision-making process is the church of All Saints, Mundesley, in north Norfolk. This originally medieval building was rebuilt in the early twentieth century, and comprises a nave with western extension, south porch, and chancel; the building is listed grade II. All the roofs are pitched and are covered with clay tiles, making them a much more obvious part of the appearance of the building, and the approach and principal views are from the south. In 2023 the church was given planning permission to change the roof covering of the chancel to natural slate including, on the south side, 'solar slates' that incorporate photovoltaic cells in a format that gives a good visual match for conventional slates in terms of size and colour.[5] The parish council and the district council climate and environment team supported the application, while the conservation officer advised it would cause harm to the significance of the building; the planning officer recommended approval on the basis that the benefit outweighed the harm, and the planning committee approved the application unanimously.

Air Source Heat Pumps

Given the widespread acknowledgement of the need to decarbonize, and with most local authorities seeking to encourage this, installing an ASHP is not of itself controversial. However, the planners will rightly be concerned with possible noise impact on neighbours, as well as the visual impact. The noise question is best addressed with a performance condition to the planning approval, which will involve measuring the typical levels of environmental noise, and (if necessary) limiting the acceptable noise from the heat pump at the most sensitive locations – for example, the nearest neighbour's bedroom window. Generally a solution will be possible, but there may be local concerns that will need managing and, once again, you will need to work with a services engineer.

EV Charging Points

This was one area where, within the Anglican system, the 2022 amendments to the Faculty Jurisdiction Rules relaxed the permission requirements so that a faculty is no longer required. The amendments address three situations:

- Installation of freestanding charging points in the curtilage (grounds) of a listed church – becomes List B.
- Installation of wall-mounted charging points on an unlisted church, hall or similar building – becomes List B.
- Installation of freestanding charging points in the curtilage of an unlisted church – becomes List A.

Each situation is accompanied by a very similar set of criteria:

- The outlet (and its support structure if freestanding) should not be higher than 1.6m from the level of the surface used for parking vehicles.
- Any new disturbance below ground level is kept to a minimum.
- The charger serves an area that may be lawfully used for off-street parking.
- The charger is not situated within 2m of a highway.
- (For freestanding chargers) No more than one upstand is provided for each parking space.
- The work is carried out by a body or person who is registered with the relevant government department or other body responsible for accreditation.

Arguing for Change

For some, the Ecclesiastical Exemption has a bad press, but I hope it is clear from what is written above that the system has a lot to recommend it. The Exemption provides a much greater understanding – at least in principle – of the life of an individual church, and the legitimacy of change to the building to accommodate the life of the Christian community in that place.

It is important, then, to understand how change to historic buildings can be justified. This comes back to the balancing of 'harm' against public benefit, which mirrors a core principle of the secular listed building consent process. In an Anglican context, sustainability is acknowledged as part of the Fifth Mark of Mission, and across the Exemption the public benefit that justifies change is understood to include the worship, ministry and mission of the church. And the Church systems and most secular authorities now generally see sustainability enhancement as a public benefit, which is a recent example of significant change.

Whichever denominational system you are working within, when preparing an application the advice is to do your homework – show the world that you not only care for your building, but that you understand its history. You will be expected to assess the heritage significance of your building and of the individual parts of it, particularly those that will be affected by your proposal. It is important that these assessments of significance are honestly made – discuss this with your professional adviser/ DAC etc. before submitting. Then, crucially, spell out to the permission-givers how your proposed changes relate to the public benefits you are hoping to achieve, in terms of worship, mission and ministry. The Church of England has useful guidance and a pro forma that churches can use. This includes the following structure of five levels for assessing the significance of the different aspects of your building:

- *High* – important at national to international levels.
- *Moderate-High* – important at regional level or sometimes higher.

- *Moderate* – usually of local value but of regional significance for group or other value (e.g. vernacular architecture).
- *Low-Moderate* – of local value.
- *Low* – adds little or nothing to the value of a site or detracts from it.

Finally, in presenting such proposals, it is helpful to root any proposed changes in the developmental story of the building. A typical church building will, after all, have changed multiple times through its history. I would argue that change is in the nature of most church buildings; it is not that all change is good, just that change should in principle be seen as normal and to be expected. Indeed, this visible story of change is often what gives these buildings their special character, it's what makes them so interesting, and in many cases it accounts for their very survival.

BALANCING BENEFIT & HARM

Churchyards and Permissions

Works to any trees that have a Tree Preservation Order placed on them require permission from your local authority; this also applies to *any* tree in a conservation area, or in the grounds of a listed building.

From a Church of England permissions point of view, some works in churchyards are List A (allowed without consultation or faculty), some are List B (requiring consultation but not faculty), and others (such as felling a tree whose trunk is more than 75mm diameter) require faculty. Note that the *planting* of trees is also a List B matter – that's because, for example, planting a tree too close to a building can cause significant damage in years to come. And all levels of permission require the church to pay due regard to the CBC guidance on trees.[6]

The key takeaway is to talk to your local authority and DAC as you develop any proposals.

PV Case Study – King's College Chapel, Cambridge

Early in 2023, King's College, Cambridge was granted both planning and faculty permissions for solar panels on the roof of its iconic Chapel.[7] While this building is not a typical parish church, it does raise some interesting and relevant issues concerning our understanding of the significance of historic buildings, and their capacity to change. Given its prominence – internationally renowned and of grade I listed status – this case inevitably sets some precedents, so it deserves some discussion.

King's College Chapel falls within the Church of England's Faculty Jurisdiction system, and therefore the College did not require listed building consent from the local authority, Cambridge City Council. However, planning permission was still required, and this was granted *against* the recommendation of the planning officers and the representations of the conservation officer. The decision reflected the political will and commitments of the councillors on the planning committee – which, of course, will vary between local authorities.

King's College Chapel (spot the PV panels ...)

What we can say is that, where there is local political support, such schemes are possible, despite concern from some heritage voices. Historic England (the government's statutory adviser on the historic environment) strongly objected to the proposals, arguing that they would harm the building's architectural significance, while SPAB (the Society for the Protection of Ancient Buildings) expressed support for the principle of the proposal, but considered the benefits did not justify the harm, and so also objected to the scheme. Historic England drew attention to the outstanding significance of King's College Chapel as a work of architecture, and to the fact that it has come to symbolize Cambridge, and was surely right to do so. But it doesn't follow that the proposed solar panels would be sufficiently harmful to outweigh the benefits. Rather, I would suggest, it is a reason *in support of* the proposals.

This case begs questions of heritage professionals. The job of Historic England, and the heritage protection system as a whole, is not to *oppose* change, but to *manage* change in order to safeguard the significance of historic buildings – that is Historic England policy. Clearly some change can be very harmful, and should be prevented; but change should never be confused with harm (though sadly it often is). In the case of this iconic building, the lead roof itself is not a major part of its architectural significance – it is barely visible, at high level and behind a perforated parapet – though this, too, was a point of contention. Yes, there are points from which the panels are visible, but these are from upper floors of neighbouring buildings, or from a considerable distance. The panels have a matt finish to limit reflections, and are uniformly dark in colour, including their edging. In this case the panels are sized to match the rhythmic bay size of the roof. In practice, once installed, very few people notice them, and the change is, of course, entirely reversible.

There is another side of the significance question. Climate change is an issue of existential significance for us all; it is the defining crisis of our times. I'm sure that all the heritage voices – those that argued against the installation and those in favour such as the CBC and DAC – accept this. The difference lies in whether you think historic buildings should be changed in this way, or whether such an installation should be fitted elsewhere. My view is that King's College deserves nothing but praise for wishing to respond to the climate crisis in this way. Precisely *because* of the Chapel's prominence, this installation has symbolic value in proclaiming that the Church, the College, Cambridge, and indeed the UK are serious about the climate crisis.

I would also argue that these proposals are good in heritage terms. It is by *changing well* that historic buildings endure, by remaining relevant within a changing culture, and therefore used, and therefore cared for. To prevent appropriate change is to do them violence, because change is in their nature. Installing solar panels on the roof of King's College Chapel is good for the building, for Cambridge and for the environment – both natural *and* historic.

In my view, King's College Chapel sets an important precedent. If permission for solar panels is possible there, then it should be possible for all sorts of other important historic buildings. The case suggests a cultural shift in response to the climate crisis – a change to what is regarded as normal – and itself should therefore encourage decision makers to view such proposals more favourably. But it certainly doesn't guarantee success elsewhere, nor will it have persuaded those who remain opposed in principle.

Regrettably, what was not discussed in the planning process was the theological argument for the relevance of the panels to the mission of the Church. This is a factor that certainly should play a prominent role in deciding listed building consent within the Ecclesiastical Exemption, but is less likely to receive its due within the secular planning system.

Notes

1 See Resources R12.
2 See Resources R12.
3 Page ii; see Resources R7.
4 See Resources R12 for link to the Town and Country Planning (General Permitted Development) (England) Order 2015, Schedule 2, Part 14, Class J.
5 North Norfolk District Council, application PF/22/1649.
6 See Resources R10.
7 Cambridge City Council, application 22/03811/FUL.

Conclusion

Taking swift action on sustainability is a clear responsibility, both for society in general, and for the Church in particular. Given the urgent need to reduce our carbon emissions, we must expect buildings to be a prominent part of that. This focus on buildings does not remove the need for us as individuals to change to a low carbon lifestyle – it must be both/and, since neither will be sufficient on its own.

But alongside these very real responsibilities, the climate crisis also presents huge opportunities for the Church, not least in terms of mission and re-engagement with our communities. In an increasingly secularized society that sees little point in the Church, there is an opportunity for Christians to provide leadership at local, regional and national levels. In the Gospels, many of those who approached Jesus in good faith did so in hope of healing for themselves or their loved ones. How great would it be if the Church was once more seen as the place to go for healing – yes, of broken lives, but also of a broken world?

It is inescapably the case that the ongoing destruction of the created order and the climate crisis are the results of the way modernized societies treat the natural world. We regard it as a resource at our disposal. We seek, through the twin tools of technology and modern science, to elevate humanity to the status of gods. Technology and science are not bad of themselves, but the effects of their employment in pursuit of our own divinity are proving increasingly calamitous. This is part of the profound challenge the climate crisis presents to the whole of our modern culture, including the Church. While some of the details of Lynn White's accusation against the Church may be simplistic (see Chapter 1), the thrust of the charge still stands – the Church has indeed been complicit in facilitating the current crisis.

The Church must, therefore, face its responsibilities and repent – literally, rethink. That rethinking will include some key aspects of our theology. In this context, 'green theology' should not be seen as a specialist interest, something that can be strapped onto the side of the existing structure of our Christian belief. Rather, because Christians for centuries have paid such scant regard to God's commitment to the created order, the climate crisis challenges us to rethink the structure of our beliefs from first biblical principles. It is high time that we come to understand humanity as belonging *within* the created order, and not in a uniquely privileged and controlling position *above* it. Again, responsibility is accompanied by opportunity.

This book has sought to address just one aspect of this much larger picture – specifically, the way we can reduce the carbon impact of our church buildings. I hope you have found it useful, and that it will help your church community to make your building(s) more sustainable. Given the role they play in shaping community, and the messages they send out to those around us, buildings are indeed an important part of the larger picture. As has already been stated, a central theme of sustainability is the interrelatedness of humanity with the natural world/created order, and on the Christian view, of both humanity and the created order with God. I hope, too, that engaging with your church building in this way will prompt a broader theological reflection, and a rebalancing of that critical triangular relationship.

Richard Bauckham ends his excellent book *Bible and Ecology* on the theme of reconciliation, comparing Paul's vision of new creation in Christ (2 Cor. 5.18–20) with John's vision of the New Jerusalem in Revelation (21.9—22.5). He suggests that each passage

> pictures our reconciliation to God – along with all creation. Reconciliation with God and reconciliation with the rest of God's creation are not alternatives but natural partners. In the end they are inseparable, as John's vision shows, and in the crises of our contemporary world both are urgent needs. The Church's 'ministry of reconciliation' today must surely

embrace both. And finding our place in the biblical meta-narrative – reconciled in Christ, on the way to the reconciliation of all things in Christ – will help to sustain hope in dark times.[1]

Amen to that!

Note

1 Bauckham, *Bible and Ecology*, p. 178. See Resources R2.

Resources

This section aims to signpost readers to a selection of links to current guidance for churches; it does not claim to be comprehensive, but will hopefully provide useful starting points for further exploration of the issues raised. The resources have been organized into 12 sections which broadly follow the flow of the book.

While the links have all been checked immediately prior to publication, over time some will inevitably break, while other resources will of course be newly created. While some of what follows is denomination-related, I would urge you to look far and wide – sustainability affects all of us, regardless of denomination or indeed religion.

R1: Sustainability – General

Cebon, David, 2022, 'Hydrogen for Heating? A Comparison with Heat Pumps', Part 1, https://h2sciencecoalition.com/blog/hydrogen-for-heating-a-comparison-with-heat-pumps-part-1/. Professor David Cebon compares two low-carbon alternatives to heat: hydrogen-powered hot water boilers and electric-powered heat pumps.

Climate Change Committee, 2023, 'Delivering a Reliable Decarbonised Power System', https://www.theccc.org.uk/publication/delivering-a-reliable-decarbonised-power-system/. Detailed report on how to achieve a national reliable, resilient, decarbonized electricity supply system.

University of California, Los Angeles. 'What is Sustainability?', https://www.sustain.ucla.edu/what-is-sustainability/. Good general discussion of sustainability.

White, Lynn, 1967, 'The Historical Roots of Our Ecologic Crisis', *Science*, 155 (3767): 1203–7. https://doi.org/10.1126/science.155.3767.1203.

World Commission on Environment and Development, 1987,
'Our Common Future', the 'Brundtland Report', https://
sustainabledevelopment.un.org/content/documents/5987
our-common-future.pdf.

R2: Theology

Anglican Communion, 'The Five Marks of Mission', https://www.
anglicancommunion.org/mission/marks-of-mission.aspx.
Bauckham, Richard, 2010, *Bible and Ecology: Rediscovering the
Community of Creation*, London: Darton, Longman & Todd.
Deane-Drummond, Celia, 2017, *A Primer in Ecotheology: Theology
for a Fragile Earth*, Eugene, OR: Cascade Books.
Habel, Norman C., ed. 2000, *Readings from the Perspective of Earth*,
The Earth Bible 1, Cleveland, OH: Sheffield Academic Press.
Marlow, Hilary, 2009, *Biblical Prophets and Contemporary
Environmental Ethics: Re-Reading Amos, Hosea, and First Isaiah*,
Oxford: Oxford University Press.
Marlow, Hilary and Mark Harris, eds, 2022, *The Oxford Handbook
of the Bible and Ecology*, Oxford: Oxford University Press.
van Montfoort, Trees, 2022, *Green Theology: An Eco-Feminist and
Ecumenical Perspective*, translated by Wim Reedijk, London:
Darton, Longman & Todd.

R3: Eco Church, Eco-Congregation, etc.

Eco Church: https://ecochurch.arocha.org.uk.
Eco Church Resources: https://ecochurch.arocha.org.uk/resources/.
Eco-Congregation: http://www.ecocongregation.org/.
Eco-Congregation Scotland:
   https://www.ecocongregationscotland.org/.
Eco-Congregation Ireland:
   https://www.ecocongregationireland.com/.

R4: Church of England – Sustainability

Contact details for diocesan environmental officers and net zero
carbon officers: https://www.churchofengland.org/about/
environment-and-climate-change/contact-details-diocesan-
environmental-officers-and-net-zero.

Energy Footprint Tool: https://www.churchofengland.org/
about/policy-and-thinking/our-views/environment-and-
climate-change/about-our-environment/energy-footprint-tool.
Allows Church of England churches to work out their 'carbon
footprint' from their utility bills.

Environment in Prayer, Worship and Teaching: https://www.
churchofengland.org/about/environment-and-climate-change/
environment-prayer-worship-and-teaching. Some Church of
England resources.

Fundraising for Net Zero Carbon and the Environment: https://
www.churchofengland.org/about/environment-and-climate-
change/fundraising-for-net-zero-carbon.

Heating: https://www.churchofengland.org/resources/
churchcare/advice-and-guidance-church-buildings/heating.
Gateway page to the ten documents listed in Chapter 4.

Net Zero Carbon Routemap: https://www.churchofengland.org/
about/environment-and-climate-change/net-zero-carbon-
routemap.

Net Zero Carbon and Environmental Case Studies: https://www.
churchofengland.org/about/environment-and-climate-change/
towards-net-zero-carbon-case-studies.

Practical Path to Net Zero Carbon: https://www.churchof
england.org/resources/churchcare/net-zero-carbon-church/
practical-path-net-zero-carbon-churches.

Renewable Energy Usage: https://facultyonline.churchof
england.org/renewables. Part of the Church Heritage Record,
this map shows current installations of renewable technologies
across all Church of England churches, searchable by
technology, diocese, listing grade; the data are not perfect (see
'Update our Renewable Energy Data' below).

Update our Renewable Energy Data: https://www.churchof
england.org/resources/churchcare/advice-and-guidance-
church-buildings/renewable-energy/update-our-renewable.
Link to update the information for the renewables map for
Church of England churches.

R5: Church of England – Sustainability Guidance Documents

'Net Zero Carbon Church': https://www.churchofengland.org/resources/churchcare/net-zero-carbon-church. Gateway page.

'Brief Guide to Biomass Boilers': https://www.churchofengland.org/sites/default/files/2021-08/CCB_Biomass_Guidance.pdf.

'Brief Guide to Electric Car Charging': https://www.churchofengland.org/sites/default/files/2023-10/cbc_ev_charging_guidance.pdf.

'Brief Guide to Lighting in Churches': https://www.churchofengland.org/sites/default/files/2022-05/CCB_Lighting_guidance.pdf.

'Brief Guide to Solar Panels and Faculty': https://www.churchofengland.org/sites/default/files/2021-09/Solar_Panels_and_Faculty_Guidance_0.pdf.

'Brief Guide to Solar Photovoltaic (PV) Panels': https://www.churchofengland.org/sites/default/files/2021-08/CCB_SolarPV_Guidance.pdf.

'Radiant Heating Trial, St Matthew's, Bristol': https://www.churchofengland.org/sites/default/files/2023-09/case_study_halo_chandelier_bristol_st_matthew.pdf.

'Reducing Embodied Carbon': https://www.churchofengland.org/sites/default/files/2023-05/Reducing_Embodied_Carbon_CCB-Guidance.pdf. Explains embodied carbon, and how to reduce it for projects in church buildings.

R6: Other Denominations, Other Resources

360° Carbon by Climate Stewards, 'Making Carbon Footprints Make Sense': https://360carbon.org/en-gb/. Easy-to-use carbon footprint calculator.

Baptist Union Environment Network: https://www.baptist.org.uk/Groups/349554/Baptist_Union_Environment.aspx.

Catholic Church of England and Wales, 'Environment': https://www.cbcew.org.uk/environment/.

Green Christian: https://greenchristian.org.uk/.

Joint Public Issues Team, 'Hope in God's Future' report: https://jpit.uk/hope-in-gods-future-2.

Methodist Church, 'Environment and Climate Change': https://
www.methodist.org.uk/action/climate/.
Operation Noah: https://operationnoah.org. Christian charity
working with the Church to inspire action on the climate crisis.
Pope Francis, Encyclical Letter *Laudato Si'*, On Care for our
Common Home, 2015, https://www.vatican.va/content/
dam/francesco/pdf/encyclicals/documents/papa-francesco_
20150524_enciclica-laudato-si_en.pdf.
United Reformed Church: Become a Greener Church: https://urc.
org.uk/your-church/church-local-and-global/greenerchurch/.

R7: Historic England Sustainability Guidance

'Adapting Historic Buildings for Energy and Carbon Efficiency'
(Historic England Advice Note 18): https://historicengland.
org.uk/images-books/publications/adapting-historic-buildings-
energy-carbon-efficiency-advice-note-18.
'Energy Efficiency and Retrofit in Historic Buildings: How to
Improve Energy Efficiency': https://historicengland.org.uk/
advice/technical-advice/retrofit-and-energy-efficiency-in-historic-
buildings/.
'Energy Efficiency and Places of Worship': https://historic
england.org.uk/advice/caring-for-heritage/places-of-worship/
making-changes/advice-by-topic/energy-efficiency/.
'Installing New Services': https://historicengland.org.uk/advice/
technical-advice/building-services-engineering/installing-new-
services/.
'Installing Solar Panels': https://historicengland.org.uk/advice/
technical-advice/building-services-engineering/installing-
photovoltaics.

R8: Technologies

Cheribim: https://www.cheribimapp.com/sensors. One source of
sensors to monitor your building, as discussed in Chapter 3.
EV charging connector types: https://www.zap-map.com/
ev-guides/connector-types. A summary of charging speed
terminology and connector types.
'Halo Church Heating at St Matthew's': https://www.herschel-
infrared.co.uk/casestudies/halo-church-heating-at-st-
matthews/. Manufacturer's case study.

'Herschel Halo Heating: Performance Review of Trial Installation at St Matthew's Church, Bristol': https://d3hgrlq6yacptf. cloudfront.net/5f3ecfb22c3ee/content/pages/documents/ cbc-halo-review-summary-v1-2.pdf. Summary report by Tobit Curteis Associates & Inspired Efficiency.

'Hydrogen and Hydrotreated Vegetable Oils': https://www. churchofengland.org/resources/churchcare/advice-and-guidance-church-buildings/hydrogen-and-hydrotreated-vegetable-oils. Church of England guidance.

Kensa Heat Pumps, 'What is a Water Source Heat Pump?': https://www.kensaheatpumps.com/water-source-heat-pump/. A manufacturer's explanation of how water source heat pumps work.

Office for Zero Emission Vehicles: https://www.gov.uk/ government/organisations/office-for-zero-emission-vehicles. Team working across UK government departments to support the transition to zero emission vehicles.

Tepeo: Zero Emission Boiler: https://www.tepeo.com/the-zeb. Example of innovative electric boiler discussed in Chapter 4.

R9: Non-mains Drainage Systems

Diocese of Canterbury, 'Non-mains Drainage Systems for Churches': https://www.canterburydiocese.org/parishsupport/ church-buildings/nonmains-drainage-systems-for-churches/. Good overview.

Elemental Solutions, 'Trench Arch Sewage Treatment': https:// www.elementalsolutions.co.uk/trench-arch-sewage-treatment/. Good context from the author of the Gloucester DAC design note.

Gloucester DAC, 'Waste Water from Churches': https:// d3hgrlq6yacptf.cloudfront.net/5f218af5bba08/content/pages/ documents/1424700436.pdf. Note this document is more than 20 years old; it is essential to read this in conjunction with more recent guidance.

Oxford Archaeology, 'Assessing the Impact of Trench Arch Drainage Systems on Archaeological Remains in Churchyards': https://historicengland.org.uk/research/results/reports/7061/ AssessingtheImpactofTrenchArchDrainageSystemson ArchaeologicalRemainsinChurchyards.

R10: Churchyards and Biodiversity

Caring for God's Acre Action Pack: https://www.caringfor
godsacre.org.uk/resources/action-pack/. Some 35 fact sheets
available as a single download, or individually. Particular
attention drawn to sheets A12 (Improving the Carbon
Footprint of Your Burial Ground), D1 (Involving Volunteers),
and D4 (Telling the Story – Interpretation).
Church of England Guidance on Trees: https://www.churchof
england.org/resources/churchcare/advice-and-guidance-
church-buildings/trees.

R11: Professional Resources

The Ecclesiastical Architects and Surveyors Association (EASA),
'Sustainability and Net Zero Carbon': https://easa.org.uk/
resources/sustainability-net-zero-carbon/. With links to the
Sustainability and Net Zero Carbon Best Practice Notes on
Quinquennial Inspection Reports and Church Projects.

R12: Permissions

Department for Culture, Media and Sport (DCMS), 2010, 'The
Operation of the Ecclesiastical Exemption and Related Planning
Matters for Places of Worship in England: Guidance': https://
www.gov.uk/government/uploads/system/uploads/
attachment_data/file/77372/OPSEEguidance.pdf.
Faculty Jurisdiction Rules: https://churchofengland.org/sites/
default/files/2024-07/faculty-jurisdiciton-rules-2015-amended-
up-to-2024.pdf.
Town and Country Planning (General Permitted Development)
(England) Order, 2015, https://www.legislation.gov.uk/
uksi/2015/596/schedule/2/part/14/made. Schedule 2, Part
14, Class J deals with solar thermal and solar PV, as discussed in
Chapter 6.
Walter, Nigel, 2023, 'The Ecclesiastical Exemption in Practice',
*Historic Churches: The Conservation and Repair of Ecclesiastical
Buildings*, 30, 17–20: https://www.buildingconservation.
com/books/churches2023/16/. Overview of the Ecclesiastical
Exemption in the UK.

Appendix: The Practical Path to Net Zero Carbon (PPNZC)

To download this document for printing at A4 size, please follow the link on the Church of England's 'Net Zero Carbon Church' page: https://www.church ofengland.org/resources/churchcare/net-zero-carbon-church.

A practical path to net zero carbon
A checklist for your church

Welcome to the Net Zero Checklist.

The Church of England's General Synod has recognised the climate emergency and called on all parts of the Church to become net zero carbon by 2030.

This commitment requires us all to take action to reduce our carbon footprint. This will involve making material changes to our buildings and adopting new behaviours that both reduce our energy use and switch usage to renewable sources.

This checklist is a tool for reviewing the carbon emissions of your church building(s) and identifying actions that can be taken to help your church reduce its energy use and associated carbon emissions. It should be used alongside the "Practical path to net zero carbon for churches" guide which provides additional advice and information to help you in this journey.

The actions recommended have been developed based on the findings of a national church energy audit programme and with input from of a range of professionals in the field. Depending on the size and complexity of your church, you may also wish to commission a specialist energy audit. Contact your Diocesan Environment Officer to find out more.

To use this checklist tool, complete the tick boxes in each section, before identifying which actions you will take as a church. The tool can be printed off or completed by clicking and typing into the pdf form.

We suggest you review progress towards implementing these actions at a PCC meeting.

If you require any support, please contact your Diocesan Environment Officer.

Please note: Many of the actions suggested in this checklist require a faculty. Please seek advice from your DAC before taking action, especially if the church interior is of historic, architectural or artistic interest; stabilising the environment for these interiors is important to minimise cycles of treatment, with their inherent carbon cost.

THE CHURCH OF ENGLAND
Environment Programme

Our collective approach to net zero is underpinned by six principles:

Well maintained

Reduce heat loss by keeping on top of basic maintenance and ensuring the building is wind and watertight. Maintain the roof and gutters, to prevent water from entering the building and warm air escaping. Fix any broken window panes and make sure opening windows shut tightly.

Buy renewable

Switch to 100% renewable electricity, for example through Parish Buying's energy basket, and 'green' gas. Whilst this does not reduce the energy you use, it means it comes from a cleaner source. It is the simplest thing you can do to cut your net carbon footprint.

Waste less

Waste less electricity, waste less gas/oil, tackle any food waste, reduce leaks and wasting water, and avoid unnecessary purchases. Read the "Practical Path to Net Zero" and "Energy Efficiency Guidance" for a wide range of ideas.

Electric not gas/oil

Burning oil and gas to heat our churches is contributing greenhouse gasses to the atmosphere. We need to 'decarbonise' our heating. Where possible, move to electric heating, using electricity that comes from 100% renewable sources. There are many options such as heat pumps, pew heaters, and infra-red panel heaters and chandeliers.

Generate more

For some churches, there are opportunities to generate electricity onsite from solar PV panels, or very occasionally wind turbines or small-scale hydro.

Offset the rest

Once you have made real reductions in your energy use, you can offset the small remaining amount through Climate Stewards or other reputable schemes to become 'net zero'. Churches with grounds can also consider if there is an area where they could let vegetation or a tree grow, as a natural way to capture carbon from the air.

2

CHECKLIST

Part A - Where do we start?

These are actions that nearly all churches can benefit from, even those primarily used only on a Sunday.

They are relatively easy and are a good place for churches to start, when trying to move towards 'net zero'.

		Already done / up-to-date	Not applicable	Not a priority right now	Explore further / get advice	Priority
The building itself:						
A1.	Maintain the roof and gutters, to prevent damp entering the building and warm air escaping.	☐	☐	☐	☐	☐
A2	Fix any broken window panes* and make sure opening windows shut tightly, to reduce heat loss.	☐	☐	☐	☐	☐
A3	Insulate around heating pipes to direct heat where you want it; this may allow other sources of heat to be reduced in this area.	☐	☐	☐	☐	☐
A4	If draughts from doors are problematic, draught-proof the gaps or put up a door-curtain*.	☐	☐	☐	☐	☐
A5	Consider using rugs/floor-coverings (with breathable backings) and cushions on/around the pews/chairs.	☐	☐	☐	☐	☐
Heating and lighting:						
A6	Switch to 100% renewable electricity (for example through Parish Buying's energy basket) and 'green' gas.	☐	☐	☐	☐	☐
A7	Match heating settings better to usage, so you only run the heating when necessary*.	☐	☐	☐	☐	☐
A8.	If you have water-filled radiators, try turning off the heating 15 minutes before the service ends; for most churches this allows the heating system to continue to radiate residual warmth*.	☐	☐	☐	☐	☐
A9.	If you have radiators, add a glycol based 'anti-freeze' to your radiator system and review your frost setting.	☐	☐	☐	☐	☐
A10.	Replace lightbulbs with LEDs, where simple replacement is possible.	☐	☐	☐	☐	☐
A11.	Replace floodlights with new LED units.	☐	☐	☐	☐	☐
A12.	If you have internet connection, install a HIVE- or NEST-type heating controller, to better control heating.	☐	☐	☐	☐	☐
A13.	If your current appliances fail, then replace with A+++ appliances.	☐	☐	☐	☐	☐
People and policies:						
A14.	Complete the Energy Footprint Tool each year, as part of your Parish Return, and communicate the results.	☐	☐	☐	☐	☐
A15.	Create an Energy Champion who monitors bills and encourages people to turn things off when not needed.	☐	☐	☐	☐	☐
A16.	Write an energy efficiency procurement policy; commit to renewable electricity and A+++ rated appliances.	☐	☐	☐	☐	☐
A17.	Consider moving PCC meetings elsewhere during cold months, rather than running the church heating.	☐	☐	☐	☐	☐

3

Offset the rest:					
A18.	For most low usage 'Sunday' churches, once they have taken steps like these, their remaining non-renewable energy use will be very small. For the majority, all they need to do now to be 'net zero' is offset the small remaining amount of energy through Climate Stewards or other reputable schemes.	☐	☐	☐	☐	☐
A19.	Also, think about your church grounds. Is there an area where you could let vegetation or a tree grow?	☐	☐	☐	☐	☐

* If interiors are of historic, architectural or artistic interest, seek professional and DAC advice first.

Part B - Where do we go next?

These actions may cost more than the ones in Part A and some will require specialist advice and/or installers.

They are often good next steps for churches ready to take the next step towards 'net zero'.

		Already done / up-to-date	Not applicable	Not a priority right now	Explore further / get advice	Priority
The building itself:						
B1.	If you have an uninsulated, easy-to-access roof void, consult with your Quinquennial Inspector (QI) about insulating the loft*.	☐	☐	☐	☐	☐
B2.	If you have problematic draughts from your door, and a door-curtain wouldn't work, consult with your QI about installing a glazed door within your porch, or even a draught-lobby*.	☐	☐	☐	☐	☐
B3.	Consider creating one or more smaller (separately heatable) spaces for smaller events.	☐	☐	☐	☐	☐
B4.	Consider fabric wall-hangings or panels, with an air gap behind, as a barrier between people and cold walls.	☐	☐	☐	☐	☐
Heating and lighting:						
B5.	Learn how your building heats/cools and the link to comfort, by using data loggers (with good guidance).	☐	☐	☐	☐	☐
B6.	Improve your heating zones and controls, so you only warm the areas you are using.	☐	☐	☐	☐	☐
B7.	Install TRVs on radiators in meeting rooms and offices, to allow you to control them individually.	☐	☐	☐	☐	☐
B8.	Consider under-pew electric heaters and/or infra-red radiant panel heaters*, which keep people warm without trying to heat the whole church space. Radiant panels are especially good for specific spaces like chapels and transepts, which you might want warm when you don't need the whole church to be warm.	☐	☐	☐	☐	☐
B9.	If you have radiators, install a magnetic sediment 'sludge' filter to extend the life of the system.	☐	☐	☐	☐	☐
B10.	Consider thermal and/or motion sensors to automatically light the church when visitors come in, for security lights, and for kitchens and WCs.	☐	☐	☐	☐	☐
B11.	Install an energy-saving device such as Savawatt on your fridge or other commercial appliances.	☐	☐	☐	☐	☐
B12.	Get your energy supplier to install a smart meter, to better measure the energy you use.	☐	☐	☐	☐	☐

4

People and policies:						
B13.	Vary service times with the seasons, so in winter you meet early afternoon when the building is warmer.	☐	☐	☐	☐	☐

* If interiors are of historic, architectural or artistic interest, seek professional and DAC advice first.

Part C - Getting to zero

These are bigger, more complex actions, which only churches with high energy use are likely to consider.

They could reduce energy use significantly, but require substantial work (which itself has a carbon cost) and have a longer payback.

They all require professional advice, including input from your DAC.

The building itself:		Already done / up-to-date	Not applicable	Not a priority right now	Explore further / get advice	Priority
C1.	Draught-proof windows*.	☐	☐	☐	☐	☐
C2.	If you have an open tower void, insulate or draught-proof the tower ceiling *.	☐	☐	☐	☐	☐
C3.	Double-glaze or secondary-glaze suitable windows in well-used areas such offices, vestries and halls*.	☐	☐	☐	☐	☐
C4.	Internally insulate walls in well-used areas such as offices, vestries and halls*.	☐	☐	☐	☐	☐
C5.	If you have pew platforms, consider insulating under the wooden platform with breathable materials*.	☐	☐	☐	☐	☐
C6.	Reinstate ceilings, and insulate above*.	☐	☐	☐	☐	☐
Heating and lighting:						
C7.	Install a new LED lighting system, including all harder-to-reach lights, new fittings and controls.	☐	☐	☐	☐	☐
C8.	Install solar PV, if you have an appropriate roof and use sufficient daytime electricity in the summer.	☐	☐	☐	☐	☐

* If interiors are of historic, architectural or artistic interest, seek professional and DAC advice first.

5

Part D - "Only if..."

These are actions which a church might undertake at specific times (such as when reordering is happening) or in very specific circumstances. They nearly all require professional advice, including input from your DAC.

		Already done / up-to-date	Not applicable	Not a priority right now	Explore further / get advice	Priority
The building itself:						
D1.	If you are reroofing anyway, then insulate the roof, if appropriate for your roof*.	☐	☐	☐	☐	☐
D2.	If you have an uninsulated wall with a cavity (typically built 1940 onwards), then insulate the cavity.	☐	☐	☐	☐	☐
D3.	If the building is regularly used and suitable, such as a church hall, consider appropriate external insulation or render, appropriate for the age and nature of the building*.	☐	☐	☐	☐	☐
Heating and lighting:						
D4.	If there's no alternative that does not run on fossil-fuels, then replace an old gas boiler or an oil boiler with a new efficient gas boiler.	☐	☐	☐	☐	☐
D5.	If yours is a well-used church which you want to keep warm throughout the week, then consider an air or ground source heat pump. Ground source heat pumps are more expensive and invasive to install than air source heat pumps, but run more efficiently once installed, depending on ground conditions.	☐	☐	☐	☐	☐
D6.	If you are doing a major reordering or lifting the floor anyway, and yours is a very regularly used church, then consider under-floor heating. This can work well in combination with a heat pump (above).	☐	☐	☐	☐	☐
Church grounds:						
D7.	If you have car parking that is sufficiently used, EV charging points for electric cars can work out cost neutral or earn a small amount of income for the church. Note, they will increase the church's own energy use, but will support the uptake of electric cars. They could be good in combination with solar PV panels.	☐	☐	☐	☐	☐

* If interiors are of historic, architectural or artistic interest, seek professional and DAC advice first.

IDENTIFYING NEXT STEPS

Checklist completed by:	Date of the PCC meeting checklist results will be reported to?
Date completed:	

A) Actions we have marked as 'Already done' which have positively impacted our carbon footprint are:

1	
2	
3	

B) **Priority Actions:**
   Identify the next step for those actions which you have marked as a priority.
   Who will be responsible for taking these forward. By when?

Action	Who's responsible?	Target date for completion	Date of review by PCC
1			
2			
3			
4			

C) **Further Actions**
   Identify any actions which you have marked as 'explore further'.
   Who will be responsible for exploring these. By when?

Action	Who's responsible?	Target date for completion	Date of review by PCC
1			
2			
3			
4			

If more space is required for creating your 'Next steps action plan', please use additional sheets or your own document template.

7

Church of England guidance and support, to help you take action:

Net zero carbon church suite of guidance
https://www.churchofengland.org/resources/churchcare/net-zero-carbon-church

Case studies
https://www.churchofengland.org/more/policy-and-thinking/our-views/environment-and-climate-change/towards-net-zero-carbon-case

Net Zero Webinars
https://www.churchofengland.org/more/policy-and-thinking/our-views/environment-and-climate-change/webinars-getting-net-zero-carbon

To calculate your carbon footprint

- Energy Footprint Tool: https://www.churchofengland.org/more/policy-and-thinking/our-views/environment-and-climate-change/energyfootprinting

- 360 Carbon: https://360carbon.org/

Sources of funding
https://www.parishresources.org.uk/resources-for-treasurers/funding/
(Section 4 "National List of Charitable Grants")

Parish Buying (for switching to green electricity, energy audits, and LED lighting)
https://www.parishbuying.org.uk/

Find your Diocesan Environment Officer
https://www.churchofengland.org/more/policy-and-thinking/our-views/environment-and-climate-change/deo-map

Your DAC Secretary
Details available via your diocesan website. Many DACs have heating and sustainability advisors, who give free advice.

External partners offering useful resources

Historic England
https://historicengland.org.uk/advice/technical-advice/energy-efficiency-and-historic-buildings/

A Rocha (Eco Church)
https://ecochurch.arocha.org.uk/

SPAB
https://www.spab.org.uk/advice/knowledge-base

© Archbishops Council January 2021.
Queries: catherine.ross@churchofengland.org Cathedral & Church Buildings Division

8

Index